LIBRARY ADMINISTRATION AND RESOURCES

R. KRISHNAMURTHY

COMMONWEALTH PUBLISHERS

Library Administration and Resources

First Published : 2026

ISBN 81-7169-456-X

Published by

COMMONWEALTH PUBLISHERS (P) LTD.
4831/24, Govind Lane,
Ansari Road, Darya Ganj,
New Delhi - 110002
Ph. : 23272541, 23242541
e-mail : commonwealthpublishers2016@gmail.com

Distributed by :

ARJUN PUBLISHING HOUSE
4831/24, Govind Lane,
Ansari Road, Darya Ganj,
New Delhi - 110002
Ph. : 23272541, 23242541
e-mail : arjunbooks2001@gmail.com

Laser Typesetting by :

Dimple Computers
Delhi

Printed at :

Roshan Digital Printers
Delhi

PREFACE

A mechanisation program in a library is a major undertaking, requiring a commitment of resources and management talent. Methods for management have been evolving as much through trial and error as through design.

Although phrased variously by different writers, the issues with which management should be concerned usually include: (a) determining objectives, (b) preparing plans for achieving the objectives, including developing cost and time schedules, (c) authorising and controlling the required work, (d) monitoring and evaluating progress towards the objectives, (e) identifying alternate corrective actions as problems develop, and (f) informing staff of the effects of the program upon them.

Among these issues, first, and perhaps most important, the library management has the responsibility of determining the objectives to be achieved by the mechanisation program, including the definition of priorities. In doing, so, the systems analysis staff may well provide a picture of present operations and future possibilities, but the ultimate decision among the alternatives must rest with management.

Editor

Contents

1

MANAGEMENT PLANNING

A mechanisation program in a library is a major undertaking, requiring a commitment of resources and management talent. Methods for management have been evolving as much through trial and error as through design. This chapter outlines some of the management considerations that should be recognised and planner for.

Although phrased variously by different writers, the issues with which management should be concerned usually include: (a) determining objectives, (b) preparing plans for achieving the objectives, including developing cost and time schedules, (c) authorising and controlling the required work, (d) monitoring and evaluating progress towards the objectives, (e) identifying alternate corrective action as problems develop, and (f) informing staff of the effects of the program upon them.

Among these issues, first, and perhaps most important, the library management has the responsibility of determining the objectives to be achieved by the mechanisation program, including the definition of priorities. In doing, so, the systems analysis staff may well provide a picture of present operations and future possibilities, but the ultimate decision among the alternatives must rest with management.

Second, the costs involved in mechanisation are so great that budgetary allocations for each stage of development and implementation must be carefully planned. Development, no matter how carefully controlled, is very likely to be delayed at a number of points. On cause, having little to do with technical problems, arises from unforeseen delays in funding. This imposes a real and important constraint on the planning process, since the development plan itself must be designed to provide for intermediate systems whose operations can be continued even if later systems must be deferred for an indefinite time.

Third, the time schedule for development must be defined by library management. Again, the systems analysis staff can provide the technical support by defining likely series of events in time, but so many issues must be reconciled-many of them essentially nontechnical in character- that the library management must ultimately determine when things are to be done.

Fourth, the management of the actual development and implementation itself rests with library management. Unfortunately, it is a kind of management relatively unfamiliar to the librarian. The work is highly technical issues involved. Furthermore, usually it is a one-time project, rather than an on-going operation such as the library itself represents. As a result, the management problems are very different from those normally encountered in library administration.

Fifth, the development of a system requires may compromises to be made among conflicting requirements and capabilities. Great care is required to avoid an overcommitment to the demands of one or another specialised interest—to those who regard the aim as effective utilisation of equipment. To those whose concern is with cost/effectiveness, to those concerned with day-to-day operations, to those with some ideal of perfection. Conflicts among these interests can be exemplified by the issues of filing rules—simple alphabetical sorting which makes for efficient machine utilisation, or cataloging code which better fits the requirements of the staff and users? Where the conflicts cannot be resolved on technical ground, library management must weight the issues involved and arrive at a judicial decision.

Sixth, a mechanised system will introduce significant changes in the relationships among the library, its staff, and its readers. The library management must therefore plan a program of education for the staff and public relations with the readers to ensure an understanding of the effects of mechanisation and acceptance of them.

This chapter introduces these issues of management planning—objectives, time schedules, and budgets; project management; training and public relations.

Before doing so, however, it seems important to establish the context within which management decisions will probably be made. Generally, it can be described in this way: Automation of library clerical processes is not a trivial problem even though, superficially, they seem to be little more than analogues of business data processed which have now been computer-based for years. There are vitally significant differences which must be recognised in management planning.

Libraries are concerned with files of truly

enormous magnitude. For example, whereas an inventory control file for a very large company might contain ten million characters, the catalog of a typical library will contain ten times as much- one hundred million characters. That of a large research library will contain over one billion characters, and the National Union Catalog has been estimated at one hundred billion characters! The conversion of such immense files into machine language is almost prohibitively expensive, but the storage and maintenance of them on a continuing basis is even more expensive—particularly since ready access to the catalog is essential.

Unfortunately, again in sharp contrast to business data processing, there is not a comparable degree of utilisation by which to justify incurring such expenditures. For example, whereas 10 per cent of a typical inventory control file will be active each day, less than 0.1 per cent of a library's catalog will be used each day. There is thus a relatively small base of activity over which to spread costs. The investment in conversion, storage, and maintenance must therefore be justified by increased benefits to a much greater extent than in business data processing. And such intangibles provide an especially difficult basis for library management planning, because of the limited discretionary resources usually available.

In fact, libraries operate on a very marginal economic basis, with remarkably small budgets for the amount of work they do. As a result, there is little of the organisational "fat' that developers of mechanised systems usually depended upon for demonstrating economies of operation.

Perhaps even more significant in management planning is the fact the library data processing involves the very substance of the library's functions. In this respect, the library's catalog, serial records, and even its circulation control files are comparable to the manufacturing component of a company and not to the bookkeeping records. Changes in the basic records of the library, which are almost certain to occur with mechanisation, therefore affect the character of the library service themselves and not simply of peripheral accounting procedures. It may be for this reason that library data processing involves a degree of intellectual judgment far beyond that in normal business data processing. For example, catalog filing rules are with good reason much more complicated than simple alphanumerical sorting. In fact, in this sense mechanising library data processing is comparable in difficulty and complexity to the development of a total management information system for a company. It is therefore especially important that management planning make adequate provision for the effects upon library service of the changes resulting from mechanisation.

Finally, library operations and their costs are relatively ill-defined, at least in the form required for mechanisation. Only recently have libraries added systems and procedures personnel to their staffs, and few libraries, even now, have procedures manuals in the detail to be found in a business. There are still relatively few people available who combine knowledge of libraries with that of data processing. Management planning therefore must recognise the necessity for adequate systems work, including procedures analysis, and accommodate the difficulties in finding or training personnel capable of doing this work.

Objectives, time schedules, and budgets

The first and most important step in the management

of a mechanisation program is the definition of objectives for it. Because program objectives must be compatible with library policies, the library administration must being by reviewing existing policies, both as documented and as generally understood. In doing so, it will probably find it necessary to develop some new policies and to document many previously undocumented ones. Then, the situation which led to the decision to undertake a modernisation program should be analysed. Typically, these might include demands for change coming from higher governing bodies; requirements for new services in response to changing conditions; increasing backlogs due to inadequate budgets, staff, or space. In any case, program objectives must be established which reflect both library policies and current or anticipated needs.

The most ambitious general objective might be the orderly development of a total system which not only exploits as many of the new technologies as possible, but does so with optimum balance of cost and effectiveness and compatibility with other (state, local, or national) library systems. A more limited one might be the documentation and analysis of existing library operations with the aim of limited improvement, through reorganisation or simplification and through limited use of proven equipment techniques and technologies. Very limited and specific objectives could include faster processing of new book orders, better control over technical processing routines, availability of more comprehensive statistic, better management information, reduction in routines performed by clerical staff, availability of better bibliographic descriptions of the collection, more effective utilisation of professional staff, improved reference services, better control over the physical collection, reduction of patron involvement in the charging transaction, and better circulation control.

In defining objectives, the librarian is confronted not only with the uses of cost and effectiveness of services as required now. He should be even more concerned with the quality and quantity of services required in the future (in 5, 10 or 15 years). Will the library, with its present means, be capable of furnishing them? What must be done so that the expected service will be made available? As a result, the librarian must make predictions and projections about the future as well as clearly understand the present roles and purposes of his library. Admittedly, the dynamic development of our educational and cultural system, together with the revolutionary developments experienced by library science in the past few years, all tend to decrease considerably one's confidence in any prediction. Nevertheless, even poor projections are better than none, and they can be revised often (perhaps once every six months) in order to maintain a reasonable, albeit minimal, degree of credibility.

For this reason, it is particularly important to develop objectives in terms of a planned progression of systems starting from the present ways of doing things and leading to some ultimates system. The importance of such an approach to library automation should not be underestimated. Libraries, as operational agencies, require that throughout development there be some level of system at all times in regular, full-scale operation in the library. Even more significant is the necessity that any interim system be capable of sustained, economic operation indefinitely. There is always uncertainty with respect to both the future and the actual progress in development of new systems. For example, related programs elsewhere and the actual availability of technology are completely outside the control of the individual library and yet essential to its planning. The progression of steps must be designed to articulate well with those programs as they actually develop,

Because of these considerations, such a progression should be planned around a logical succession of systems which perform essentially the same functions but at increasing levels of sophistication. It may therefore frequently be desirable that less sophisticated objectives be met first, as the basis on which later systems are built. Only in this way can the library avoid the pitfalls of overcommitment to some ultimate concept, on the one hand, and of a refusal to proceed (because "new machinery will soon appear") on the other.

The management planning task, assisted by the library systems analysis staff, is to delineate those functions which are to be served at each stage in the progression. Some of them will simply be continuations of existing function, unchanged in any substantial way. Others will represent significant changes- such as a book catalog replacing a card catalog. Still others will represent totally new services-perhaps mechanised information retrieval or facsimile transmission. And some will represent the need to interface with other libraries.

The criteria used in this planning process include: (a) the economic value to be expected from including, changing, or even deleting functions, (b) the logical progression in conversion from an existing function to another, more sophisticated one (e.g. in transition from a card catalog to a computer produced book catalog to an on-line computer catalog), (c) the need to relate with others in other libraries, (d) the availability of budget and personnel, (e) the availability and reliability of the necessary hardware and software

(f) the flexibility and ease of change, (g) the consistency with the ultimate objectives.

We have already commented on the necessity to define a planned progression of stages. Each of them must satisfy a clearly delineated set of requirements, appropriate to the available technology and knowledge of how to do things; each of them must embody an equally well defined set of administrative and operational control; and each should be carefully planned so as to be consistent with the ultimate objectives. But each of them must also be based upon equally well-defined financial considerations. The basis of financial support therefore should as well planned as the technical implementation of hardware and software.

In particular, cost/effectiveness measures of performance should be the primary basis for evaluation, and the decision about whether to automate in large part should be based on a comparison of cost of manual versus machine methods. While cost/effectiveness is especially difficult to evaluate when it is applied to systems development which progresses through a number of stages, spread over a period of years, this merely serves to emphasise the importance of a carefully planned progression of steps as an integral part of the development program.

Project management

The process of development and implementation of a mechanised library system is complicated and involves a large number of people. Therefore, the management of this effort must also be planned in advance, the tasks that are to be carried out assigned to development staff, and time estimates established for each task with target dates for their start and finish.

The process of creating any mechanised processing system involves the performance of activities in a series of phases, commonly used in describing and planning computer work in both government and industry. They represent a natural sequence for development of mechanised library systems as well.

1. Feasibility analysis.
2. Requirements specification.
3. Detailed design.
4. Computer programming and check-out.
5. Computer program functional test.
6. Installation and implementation.
7. Maintenance.

Each of the seven phases encompasses a set of tasks, which culminate in milestones, or concluding events. The successive completion of them becomes an objective measure of progress achieve.

Phase 1—feasibility analysis. Based on a statement of the library's requirements, an estimate must be made of the resources required for the project. A summary project plan must be prepared, and a cost-versus-benefits comparison made. During this step, the level of analysis of the library's operating system is only that absolutely necessary for cost estimation and preliminary planning purposes.

Tasks: Assemble documentation on library policies and practices.

Determine necessary development activities, including number and identify of any subsidiary efforts.

Estimate development costs for each step or task.

Check reasonableness of estimates.

Perhaps summary budget plan for development.

Estimate costs of both existing and proposed systems.

Prepare cost-benefits evaluation of the proposed application.

Phase 2—requirements specification. This step consist of the detailed study of the existing library system, and the formulation of the operational requirements for the proposed system.

Tasks: Determine library's system requirements in detail.

Analyse library's environment including projects with which it must be compatible.

Determine needed computer program characteristics.

Compare with similar systems.

Prepare performance specifications.

Assure concurrence of library policy-makers with system performance specifications.

Phase 3—detailed design. Based on the requirements specification, this step proceeds to the definition of detailed design for both the computer system and the library personnel involved. It results in documents that detail the functions to be programmed as well as the operating procedures for personnel.

Tasks: Interpret requirements specification in terms of specific equipment, volume of activity, response times, and operating environment. Review available software.

Analyse decision to "make or buy"

Revise specifications as necessary to conform with decision.

Produce a system flow diagram.

Define interfaces with other activities in the library or in other libraries.

Specify computations, logical manipulations, and transformations within each part of the library function to be done by the machine.

Design the formats and organisation of all forms and files, including machine stored records.

Develop requirements for editing, formatting, storing, and updating of the machine stored records.

Produce documentation of the detailed design.

Define test requirements.

Indoctrinate programming personnel.

Phase 4—computer programming. Based upon the detailed design specifications this step proceeds with all work necessary to produce, document, and test computer programs. Included are such activities as flow charting, coding, integration of individual programs into a program system, preparation of test data bases, detecting and correcting errors, compiling or assembling operating programs, and listing of code. It results in a completed computer program end product, tested for conformity with detailed specification.

Tasks: Flow chart each component computer program.

Specify all input and output forms.

Write programs from detailed flow charts or other program design documentation.

Compile and check program code, and make necessary error corrections.

Test the performance of each individual program and of the total program system.

Phase 5—computer program functional test. This step covers demonstration tests of the computer program system, for the library management, usually in a simulated environment at the library. Included is conduct of the demonstration tests (based on test plans prepared as a part of Phase 3, above) and analysis of the rest results. All necessary work to remedy design deficiencies revealed by these tests should be charged to the appropriate previous steps. The results should be a computer program that is proven to be in conformance with the detailed design specifications and accepted by library management.

Tasks: Conduct test according to plan.

Analyse test results.

Initiate any modifications needed for computer programs.

Document test results.

Phase 6—installation and implementation. This step covers all work necessary to install the system at the library. It includes training as well as activities for conversation from the existing manual operation.

Tasks: Prepare documentation for library staff.

Supervise conversion of data required to make system operations.

Develop training plan for library staff.

Conduct training program.

Phase 7—maintenance. System maintenance is

required for improving, changing, and correcting operational computer programs. Revisions are need because operations requirements are continually changing during the both the development and operation of the system. Although operational needs are projected during requirements analysis, in most cases they can be neither totally defined nor totally implemented in the imposed time schedules. Also, corrections must usually be made to the computer programs because errors and operational deficiencies not detected in the routine testing of the programs are usually discovered when the system becomes operational. Much of the work of program maintenance personnel must be devoted to the handling of emergencies; the remainder to modifications required to meet environmental changes.

Tasks: Develop maintenance plan and organisation.

Provide continuing communication between library operating staff and computer programmers,

Establish change procedures.

Process system changes.

Work breakdown structure

The formulation of such a comprehensive program is perhaps best accomplished by the definition of a work breakdown structure and an associated cost accounting structure. The work breakdown structure shows the component tasks of a library development project in detail and, as a basic for effective program planning, it insures that no major program activity is overlooked. It provides graphic representation of the relationship of the various components of a complex program to each other and the achievement of stated program objectives. Finally, it provides a convenient means for monitoring progress towards achieving the objectives of a program.

The work breakdown structure presented in Figure 1 illustrates how a typical major development program at a large research library might be dissected into detailed component parts. In this example, the total library system has been subdivided into three major subsystems, each of which has then been further divided in to more detailed modules, which represent work of a manageable size for program control. Each such module will then call for tasks within each of the seven phases in development, as have been outlines above in the description of those phases. In summary, the work breakdown structure produces a classification of work as follows: The library system is analysed into subsystems, each of which is analysed into modules; the work for each module is analysed into phases, with tasks specified for each phase.

Figure 1: Work breakdown structure

	Time scheduled for each phase						
	Feasibility	*Specification*	*Design*	*Programming*	*Test*	*Implmentation*	*Maintenance*
A. Technical services subsystem							
1. Selection and order-module							
2. Cataloging module							
3. Preparation module							
4. Collection control module							
5. Serials module.							

B. Reader services subsystem
   1. Circulation module
   2. Reference module
   3. Interlibrary loan module
   4 Information retrieval module

C. Library management subsystem
   1. Accounting module
   2. Personnel module
   3. Procedures control module.
   4. Management information module
   5. Inventory control module

[Time estimates would be made for each module through each phase and for each task in each phase]

Definition and control of schedule

Various analytical tools have been developed to control activities of this kind. One example is the PERT chart, essentially a flow chart tied to the work breakdown structure, in which the time dimension plays an especially important role. It has particular value in helping to determine the sequence of events which represent the longest delay in project schedule, called the *critical path* in the development.

The mechanics of preparing a PERT diagram are relatively simple. The next step is to determine the activities required for the completion of each of them and to specific milestone events by which to measure progress. Then dependencies among the individual tasks and corresponding milestone events must be identified. That is, the initiation of each activity will require the completion of one or more prior activities. These time dependencies can be visualised as a sequence, from lift to right, of the corresponding events, with arrows going to an event from all prior events necessary for its initiation.

The real value of the PERT chart lies in the use of estimates of the time required for the completion of each activity. Usually, these estimates are expressed as both a range (from most optimistic to most pessimistic) and an expected, or most likely value. When such estimates have been developed for each activity, an elapsed-time analysis can be produced by adding together all the estimated times for completion of the progression of activities and determining for each event the cumulated elapsed time to that point. Where several sequences of activities converge on a single event, the sequence (called the critical path) requiring the longest period of time determines when the corresponding activity can be initiated. In other words, all sequences of activities upon which an activity depends must be completed before that activity can be commenced. Those sequences leading up to an event which require less time than the critical path will have slack time (waiting time) built into them. This can be used for adjusting schedules so as to concentrate effort on other tasks or to minimise peak manpower, equipment, or facilities loading.

When the elapsed time analysis is complete it may be determined that the total elapsed time estimated for the program is incompatible with the required program completion date. If this happens, it will be necessary to reinspect the program logic in an effort to identify activities originally planned to occur in sequence which can, in fact, occur in parallel. Such a change in the plan, however, will almost always imply an increased risk of failure to perform as planned. Sometimes it will be possible to compensate for the increased risk by adding additional backup efforts or by assigning the same activity to two different groups for simultaneous, parallel performance. Upon closer scrutiny it may be found that some of the activities originally thought essential are, in face, only desirable and can be eliminated from the plan entirely. Eventually, this strategy will force the planned program elapsed time to be compatible with the program completion date specified by the program manager.

Next, it is necessary to analyse each week of activity in the planned program to determine what level of manpower or special facilities will be required. This may reveal, for example, that during the first weeks of the program there are heavy demands being made on various categories of manpower, and that later in the program there are periods when practically no demand is made for the same categories of manpower. It usually is possible to minimise the peaks by shifting some of the activities to later times when fewer demands are being made.

Cost accounting and control

An integral part of the planning function involves the budgeting and control of funds required for the various program activities. A convenient structure for doing so is the work breakdown structure itself. During later stages in the planning, all of the specific activities required to accomplish program objectives will be identified as tasks in the work breakdown structure. Each of the tasks (or portions of a task) may in turn be assigned a cost account number for which funds may be budgeted.

The cost account structure is used in implementing cost accounting routines. Each increment of cost (man-hours or materials dollars) is posted periodically against each of the cost account numbers. The individual elements are added together in such a way as to provide cumulative cost records at each of the summary levels in the cost account structure. At the highest level in the structure the total cumulative cost for the entire program is summarised. This number is plotted on a program status chart and monitored closely by program management. Any significant deviations of actual cost or performance from the planned cost/performance curve is the signal to program management to initiate appropriate corrective action.

Education and public relations

Among the most important activities which should be included in project planning is the education of both staff and users in the operation, implications, and effects of the system. It is necessary for several reasons.

First, staff are rightly concerned about the effects which automation will have on them personally. Unless they have a sense of involvement, this concern can turn into outright fear and antagonism. A well-planned program of education, scheduled to proceed in parallel with the development project can help overcome this concern.

Second, the staff will need to change many of the ways in which they have carried out their assigned tasks. Some of those tasks themselves may even change. In principle, the procedures manuals and task descriptions generated as part of the programming work during development are sufficient to show each staff member how work should be performed. In fact, of course, intensive training is usually required, if only to show each person how his work relates top the system as a whole. In this respect, it must be recognised that while automation of clerical processes may not change the basic professional content of librarianship, it will change much of the detail. Even professionals, therefore, will need to see why these changes may be necessary and how they relate to the major objectives.

Third, and directly related to the second reason, is the fact that many times only the staff is really in position to recognise a serious flaw in an operating procedures. Unless they have been given the opportunity to see what the purposes are, they can hardly begin to bring out what would otherwise be only intuitive feelings that "something's not right".

Fourth, any change of system (even from one manual method to another one) is bound to produce temporary traumas. Failures, changes from the familiar, bruises to esthetics- all are bruises to occur, if only because something is new. Since this is the case, particular care must be taken to prepare both staff and readers for these traumatic effects. This means that not only is a program of education needed, but public relations as well.

Orientation of library staff

it is therefore very important for the library administration to plan and carry out a careful program of orientation. It must make the staff knowledgeable about what the equipment coming into the library will do and what their own part will be in the new system. Only then will they be willing and able to participate with personal interest in successful operation.

Fortunately, time is great factor which contributes

to the ease adjustment to the encroachment of the machine. Automation does not take place from Friday night to Monday morning. The library administrator can take advantage of the year or two or even three that the development will require to get his staff actively involved. And this should not be a voluntary involvement, left to the discretion of "interested" personnel, which ignores the very person who most needs to be drawn into the activity.

It is especially important to inform staff from the time of their first awareness of the planning for a change in system. The decision to introduce a new system is made only after extensive analysis of the impact which the new equipment and system will have on the library's interests. By the same token, the employee is just as anxious to learn what impact the new system is likely to have on his interests. Frank and open discussions by management are therefore necessary to reduce rumors that otherwise may give a distorted view of the situation.

A well-planned information policy throughout the organisation has advantages even after a commitment is made to obtain equipment. If the introduction of a new system is tactfully presented, it can generate pride and satisfaction in the organisation, but the program should not be oversold or potential difficulties minimised. The important point is the realisation by management that all employees need complete and accurate facts.

It should be apparent therefore that an orientation program requires intensive and careful planning comparable to that carried on for the other aspects of the development and installation. The different requirements of various types of library staff and users for information about the system must be considered. Appropriate techniques must be developed for the dissemination of necessary types of information. The procedures for conducting the orientation must avoid interfering with on-going operations.

The first step should be to get the staff acquainted with automated data processing in general. Such indoctrination could commence with a tour of an existing computer facility, preferably one associated with a library. A special course in data processing, with emphasis on applications within the library itself could be organised. Certain of the library staff could be sent to special training schools operated by the equipment suppliers.

Once the library personnel are somewhat familiar with data processing, the professional staff should be involved in planning the introduction of automation to their respective departments. In this manner, they will see the project in terms of their own needs and will be motivated to plan and execute it well.

A pilot operation in progress in the library provides a means by which the characteristics of the system can be even more easily studied by other operating personnel. Furthermore, if the response of the personnel directly involved with the pilot operation has been favourable (and such attitudes are typical) these people can be counted on to sell the system to other people who will be working with it. In some cases it may even be possible to provide some on-the-job training in the pilot operation prior to the full implementation of the new system. Descriptions presented on the spot while touring through the library can help individuals visualise the characteristics of the new system. Other techniques can be used to maintain a high level of interest in the new system during the time just preceding the installation. Appropriate posters, demonstrations of new equipment or techniques, as well as lectures and directed reading can stimulate continued interest in the new system.

The installation phase is critical since at that time the majority of the library staff are exposed for the first time to the system as an operational entity. This is a period in which the basic attitudes of personnel who must operate and depend upon the system are solidified. If negative attitudes are established. If the users do not acquire confidence in the system, if they are less than cooperative in ensuring that the system accomplishes its goals, if they reject the system out of hand and refuse to use it, the result may be disaster from both the users' management and the developer's points of view. Such disasters and do happen. They can be prevented if appropriate steps are taken as part of the development planning to ensure the psychological acceptance of the system by the users.

2

THE DYNAMICS OF ORGANISATION

Perspectives on organisation

There are many ways of looking at organisations. When an individual starts a new job, for example, he or she needs to explore several different aspects of the organisation's workings-its dynamics:

- What is the organisational hierarchy? How does the job fit in to the 'organisation chart'—the diagram showing lines of command linking, through levels of responsibility and delegated authority, all the jobs in the organisation.
- How are decisions made? What is the mechanism (for example, through a cycle of interlocking formal meetings)? What is the style-how much autonomy do individuals have on various levels of the hierarchy? How much consultation and participation in decision-making is there?
- How do communications 'flow' within the organisation? Are they primarily written, or verbal? At a distance or face to face? 'Top down' or 'bottom up'?
- What informal networks are there? How does the 'grapevine' work? Who are the 'gate-keepers' who receive and pass on information informally? Are there equivalents of the 'King's Parade'—informal

forums where information is exchanged and deals are done? How important—how powerful—is this 'hidden' organisation?

- What is the style and 'feel' of the organisation? What are the values it projects?

This checklist (by no means complete) illustrates a number of key points about organisations. There will be an explicit formal structure—but there will also be a 'hidden' informal complex of networks. There will be agreed mechanisms (for decision-making and communication), but there will also be a strong human dimension affecting the operation of these mechanisms. As well as issues of structure, the newcomer has to assimilate the 'culture' (style, 'feel', values) of the organisation.

Organisations, then, are complex and dynamic entities. To analyse the various dimensions of this multifaceted concept, the study of organisations has drawn on a range of different perspectives. These can be presented in an historical and dialectic sequence of *thesis, antithesis* and *synthesis.*

Theories of organisational behaviour grew, initially, out of the Industrial Revolution and the development of the factory system. The classic statement of this early approach was Frederick Taylor's *Principles of scientific management* which advocated the application of 'scientifically' deduced methods to the production process. Taylor's recognition that manufacturing processes can be systematically analysed and divided into a sequence of single tasks led to time-and-motion studies and the 'assembly line' concept. 'Scientific' management viewed the organisation from an engineering perspective generally described as 'mechanistic'—the organisation as machine. This provides the initial thesis of organisational theory.

However, this approach takes little account of the human dimension. People were seen as cogs in the machine, motivated by material rewards, and told what to do by management. An emphasis on 'human relations', emerging from the perspectives of social and behavioural sciences, provides the antithesis of this view.

The classic starting-point for the 'human relations' school is the so-called 'Hawthorne effect'. A series of experiments were conducted in the Western Electric Company's factory at Hawthorne, near Chicago, between 1924 and 1932. These were intended-in the manner of scientific management-to explore the relationship between working conditions (levels of lighting, structure of the working day, etc.) and productivity. What was discovered, however, was that production increased, not because of changed working conditions, but because the workers felt important and appreciated as the subject of scientific study. The 'Hawthorne effect' is the effect of making people feel special. It underpins the maxim already quoted that 'People who feel good about themselves produce good results'.

This approach stresses the importance of individual psychology and social interaction. Motivation, the importance of peer-group relationships, the informal, 'hidden' networks of the organisation— the dynamics of the organisations are analysed in terms of interpersonal relations.

Two examples have already been used, showing the insights that can result from the application of social/behavioural sciences to management studies. One is Mintzberg's research into the nature of a manager's work. The other is Pettigrew's research into the political dimension of organisational decision-making.

A number of studies offer a contrast-an implicit comparison of thesis and antithesis-between a 'scientific management' approach and a 'human relations' approach. Best known of these studies are three published in the early 1960s:

- McGregor's Theories X and Y.
- Likert's four-stage model of management styles.
- Blake and Mouton's management grid.

Douglas McGregor contrasts two theories (which he terms 'X' and 'Y') about people in organisations. Theory X suggests:

- most people dislike work and will avoid it if possible.
- most people must, therefore, be pressured externally (persuaded, rewarded, punished, controlled) in order to get them to contribute towards organisational objectives.
- most people prefer to be led and directed, wish to avoid responsibility, have relatively little ambition, and are motivated by a need for security.

Theory Y suggests:

- people have within them the capacity for self-motivation and the potential to seek out and take on responsibility.
- people work best in a supportive environment which integrates personal goals and organisational objectives.

A manager who has 'theory X' assumptions about the

workforce is likely to take a 'scientific management' task-centered, directive approach. A manager inclined to the 'theory Y' viewpoint is likely to operate in a more people-orientated, participative, 'human relations' manner.

Rensis Likert distinguished four types of management style. The first two are authoritarian, one autocratic and exploitative, the second more benevolent. With these styles, the organisational structure is tall and narrow with centralised decision-making and little delegation. Likert's third style is consultative. Staff are asked their opinions which may, or may not, be taken into account when decisions are made. The fourth style is genuinely participative with the work group sharing their views and making decisions collectively.

The 'managerial grid' developed by Robert Blake and Jane Mouton provides a framework within which to compare the relative value given by a manger to 'concern for people' and 'concern for production'. At the end of the latter scale is an overriding concern for output and efficiency. At the end of the former scale is a 'country club' approach with comfortable personal relations, a relaxed pace of work, and low concern for output. The '1.9' position (the 'country club' approach) is excessively orientated towards human relations. The '9.1' position (concern for output above all) is excessively mechanistic. A midpoint on the grid shows a 'middle of the road' approach ensuring adequate output and satisfactory morale. A high score on both scales (the so-called '9.9' position) indicates an excellent performance in terms of both interpersonal relations and work output.

Management style is often described in terms of a continuum of possibilities from autocratic to democratic-from authoritarian to participative. In reviewing work done in this area, Charles Handy uses the more useful distinction between structuring and supportive styles. This less emotive terminology gives a positive value to both types of approach. Structure, direction, clear mechanisms and a focus on the job to be done are needed; so too is support for the individual, and awareness of social processes, and recognition of the 'psychological contract' between individual and organisation.

There is, then, a need for synthesis between the 'mechanistic' perspective and the 'social/behavioural' perspective. This is currently provided by the 'systems' approach to organisations. The perspective here is partly biological or ecological-the organisation seen as an organism, evolving and adapting as a result of internal and external stimuli-and partly that of systems theory as developed in computing and cybernetics.

The organisation is seen as a system consisting of two principal subsystems. The 'technical' subsystem incorporates the 'mechanistic' elements: plant and machinery, work-flow, routines and processes, etc. The 'social' subsystem includes the 'human relations' dimension. Both co-exist and management must give due regard to both.

The standard representation of an organisation as system includes inputs, processes, outputs and a 'control' loop providing feedback on outputs in order to regulate and adapt inputs and processes. However, organisations do not have built-in mechanisms of feedback and control, as do certain machines. Nor do they have automatic processes of adaptation and evolution, as do animals and other organisms.

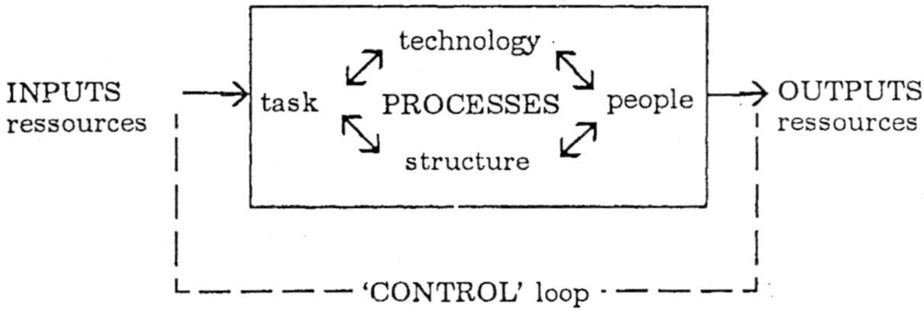

Figure 1: The organisation as system

Organisations need to introduce sophisticated communications systems in order to simulate this feedback/control/adaptation process. A central point in Peter Drucker's Innovation and entrepreneurship is the importance of information flow into and within the organisation. Drucker notes that the model of technology has shifted from mechanical processes to biological processes organised around information. There is currently considerable interest in the nature of organisations as information systems, from the perspective of computing and cybernetics (that is, the science of systems of control and communications; in particular, study of the human control system of nervous system and brain, and experimentation with applications of computing technology to intelligent processes).

The systems approach implies two important points. The first is that an organisation is a dynamic, changing entity. It is never static. An organisation chart may appear to show a fixed structure, but a fixed framework still allows for considerable freedom and flexibility of organisational behaviour-and the structure itself will adapt over time. The second is that there is no one 'best' form of organisation. Rosemary Stewart sees the major contribution of social sciences to the understanding of organisations as being this awareness: 'that different types of behaviour need different forms of organisation and that the appropriate kinds of organisation can change with the company's situation'.

This 'contingency' theory-that is, the theory that the nature of an organisation is contingent upon its situation-reinforces the importance of information. Tom Lupton (who has made a particular study of the impact of social science theories on management) points out:

> Any theory about design which rests on the principle 'it all depends' is bound to be more complex than one which rests on supposedly universally applicable injunctions. To accept a 'contingent' theory as a practical guide is to face the challenge of identifying and measuring the contingent factors.

The 'systems' approach and the concept of the 'adaptive' organisation (that is, the organisation as open system or organism, adapting to meet changing circumstances) is very relevant to libraries. As organisations, libraries clearly illustrate the coexistence of technical and social subsystems. In terms of service delivery these concepts are formalised in the traditional structural division, in academic libraries, between 'technical services' (relatively mechanical - and nowadays often automated- processes of acquisition, cataloguing, circulation control and so on) and 'reader services' (services involving the social process of interaction between staff and customers).

The library needs to be 'adaptive' given a context of discontinuous change. The customer community, the library's governing framework, and a range of external considerations all form 'contingent factors' to be taken into account.

Finally, libraries, like other adaptive organisations, need good information systems. These are necessary partly because of the point mentioned by Lupton-in order to adapt to contingencies, an organisation needs a continuous flow of information about the contingent factors surroundings it. They are also necessary as feedback/control mechanisms. The pressure of accountability requires that management demonstrate efficient use of resources, effective service delivery, and value to the customer.

Changes in size, new patterns of service provision, and the impact of information technology have all produced a considerable amount of restructuring of library organisations in recent years. Many public library departments in the UK have been restructured into larger directorates-of leisure, recreation, education, culture, etc. An emerging pattern in some British and American higher education institutions is the linking of library services with computer services to provide one integrated support network of information systems and services. In schools and colleges, libraries have, in many instances, become part of a wider structure of 'learning resources'.

These changes in size reflect changes in the pattern of service provision: each is designed to provide a clearer direction and focus. So, in theory, the fundamental purpose of a UK public library within a 'leisure' ethos is distinct from that of a public library in 'education'—although, in practice, sharp distinctions in public library service, arising from their directorate contexts, are not yet evident. In educational establishments, however, there is a clearer link between this organisational restructuring and the nature and purpose of library service. The concept of the library as a 'learning resource', for example, gives structural reinforcement to the view that a school or college library is the 'foundation of the curriculum'—a central part of the educational process, providing resources to enable students to develop learning skills.

In public libraries, the link between structural change and the pattern of service provision is more at 'grass roots' level than directorate level, with the development of the 'community librarian' approach. Sheila Ritchie links the community-orientated approach to service with a consequent need to restructure the library organisation. Ritchie contrasts a passive, building-based approach to service with a more pro-active, developmental approach which gets much closer to the customer community and seeks to meet need as well as expressed demand. The latter, she suggests, requires a decentralised structure with participative decision-making, 'bottom up' communication, and delegated authority. Her implication is that the passive, building-based approach is delivered through a centralised structure with management mechanisms which are essentially 'top down'.

An important point here is the distinction between geographic decentralisation and managerial decentralisation. Public library structures have always been decentralised to a degree, provided through a geographic scatter of branch libraries. However, the management structure has often remained highly centralised with branch librarians having very little real delegated authority. Indeed, the term 'branch library' is a literal statement of the management structure-the library as the local branch of a centrally-determined service.

In England, some local authorities-particularly some London boroughs-are developing a decentralised approach to services which are not, traditionally, delivered directly at local level: social services, for example, or housing repairs. Islington, for instance, is evolving a pattern of 'Neighbourhood Offices', each serving a local population of between 4,500 to 8,000 people. By bringing services to this 'neighbourhood' level, the local authority hopes to avoid the problems which are often attributed to centralised services-inefficiency, remoteness, inaccessibility, lack of responsiveness. In order to do this, the 'neighbourhood' concept does not just decentralise service delivery, it also decentralises management authority. Each Neighbourhood Office, and service department within that Office, has a considerable degree of autonomous authority for decision-making and resource allocation. Indeed some local authorities, including Islington, are developing mechanisms for involving local residents, directly, in decision-making at neighbourhood level.

As well as changes in size and in patterns of service delivery, changes in technology are also having an impact on the structure of library organisations. In order to take full advantage of technological opportunities there is a need to build 'systems' skills into the management team. The automation of 'housekeeping' processes and technical services can mean a reduction in the number of staff employed in these areas. The possibilities for the development of new, IT-based, services can mean the emergence of new elements in the organisation chart-staff responsible for online searching, database creation (for example, the provision of community information using videotex), or the 'repackaging' of information into state-of-the-art reports, current awareness bulletins and SDI services.

Technology may affect the process of communication between staff as well as the staffing structure. Networking and electronic mail offer opportunities for improved interactive communications across a geographically scattered organisation and this may have an impact on participation in the decision-making process.

Technology raises a further issue which has an impact on the structure of library organisations; the balance between what is provided from within the organisation and what is contracted out to external agencies. Much of the 'behind the scenes' work of processing and cataloguing, for example, is no longer carried out within libraries. It is handled externally by bibliographic cooperatives (cataloguing) and commercial suppliers of library stock (processing). Indeed, some commercial suppliers are now offering a full range of bibliographic services including facilities for stock editing and collection development. There is thus no longer any need for a large section of the organisational structure to be devoted to bibliographic services and stock processing.

Similarly, electronic publishing and document delivery is changing the structure of reference/information services. Online information, interlending networks and facsimile transmission are-to a varying degree in different types of library-replacing or supplementing library holdings of printed books and other documents. Again, the balance changes between what is directly provided (in printed form) and services which enable the library to gain access (electronically) to information held elsewhere. Structural change in the balance between 'providing' and 'enabling' is becoming a highly significant issue for public libraries in the UK as the government extends the application of compulsory tender testing to local authority services.

This discussion of current structural issues illustrates three key points. The first is that a 'structure' cannot be regarded as a fixed and unchanging framework. Changes in size, service provision, technology, the balance between 'providing' and 'enabling'—all are 'contingent factors' which impact on and influence the library's evolving structure.

The second is that an organisation's 'structure' serves a number of purposes. The organisation chart indicates the reporting structure-the lines of command (of authority and accountability) necessary in order to coordinate and control the work of the organisation. Another diagram might be needed to indicate lines of communication-for example, the horizontal lines of communication between staff on the same management level but in different parts of the organisation which will not be shown in hierarchical lines of command.

As well as coordination/control and communication, the structure needs to incorporate a 'development' dimension, if service delivery is to be pro-active and customer orientated. A further diagram might be needed to indicate the ways in which people come together in order to plan service and think ahead.

The third point is that these purposes are sometimes, seemingly, in conflict. Consider the following checklists:

coordination	division
control	delegation
accountability	autonomy
stability	innovation
conformity	creativity.

These are all desirable characteristics. The work need to be divided up in an appropriate manner-yet it also needs to be coordinated and integrated to a common

purpose. In order to get 'close to the customer' there is a need to delegate authority so that staff dealing directly with customers have some autonomy-yet there is a need to provide mechanisms for overall control and accountability to senior management. A pro-active and 'adaptive' organisation will wish to support innovation and creativity-yet there has also to be a measure of stability and conformity to accepted procedures, agreed objectives and shared values. Essentially, this is a conflict between elements of centralisation and decentralisation. A major challenge for those library managers involved in any restructuring exercise is to keep these elements in balance.

The lines of command and the characteristics expressed in the left-hand checklist (above) operate through hierarchy and bureaucracy. The hierarchy enables everyone in the organisation to know to whom they are accountable and for whom they are responsible. The bureaucracy lays down rules and procedures.

The hierarchy expressed the levels of power and authority from Chief Executive to the bottom rung on the corporate 'ladder'. The following illustrates how this reporting structure might look for a library assistant in a public and an academic library:

Library Assistant	Library Assistant
↓	↓
Branch Librarian	Assistant Librarian
↓	↓
Area Librarian	Sub-Librarian (i.e. Section Head)
↓	↓
Deputy Librarian	Deputy Librarian
↓	↓
Chief Librarian	Chief Librarian

In both (rather simplified) cases, the hierarchy has five levels; the Chief and Deputy as senior management; the Area Librarian or 'Sub-Librarian' (a curious term used in UK universities) as middle management; and the Branch Librarian or Assistant Librarian as junior, line management.

One of the challenges of organisational structure is to keep the line of command as short and tight as possible by reducing to a minimum the number of levels in the hierarchy. This is a challenge because of the need to keep each individual manager's 'span of control'—the number of people for whom that manager is responsible-within manageable proportions. In the example above it might be possible to remove from the public library hierarchy the middle-management level of Area Librarian, but all the Branch Librarians would then report directly to senior management. This is fine in a relatively small public library organisation. But if the organisation is large-say, of four areas each containing six branches-then the Deputy and Chief would have 24 Branch Librarians reporting directly to them. In terms of the span of control it would probably be more effective to retain the Area Librarians.

There is, then, a need to consider three points when examining the hierarchy of an organisation

- overall size of the organisation
- levels in the hierarchy
- spans of control for individual managers.

A fourth point which has a crucial impact on organisational structure-and which relates to the right-hand checklist (division, delegation, etc.)—is the need to divide the work to be done into a number of departments. Traditionally, there are four ways in which this can be done.

- by function
- by product
- by territory
- by customer group.

The classic division of public library work is by function-reference, lending, bibliographic services, etc.- and by territory, though a structure of branch libraries. In academic libraries there will be an element of functional division (bibliographic services, interlibrary loan, circulation desk, etc.) and also some division by customer group with the establishment of subject-based departments within the library. Public libraries also divide work on the basis of customer groups; traditionally with the division between adult and children's services and, more recently, with the targetting of services to particular customer groups- elderly people, unemployed people, people from particular minority ethnic groups, etc. Finally, there is also some division by product-for example, music libraries, community information services, current awareness bulletins, etc. The fact that libraries use all four ways of dividing work into departments illustrates the complexity of library organisations and the difficulty of finding a structure which integrates all elements to meet service objectives.

Departmental separatism-by which the organisation fragments into several departments which rarely communicate with each other-can be a characteristic of large library systems. There is no real communication between 'central' and 'the branches', between sites or subject libraries, between technical and reader services, etc. Equally, it can be experienced by the library itself in its relations with the other parts of the parent organisation. In some large corporations, the library can appear by passed and marginalised as the web of corporate communications and decision-making processes seems not to include the library staff.

There are a number of ways by which departmental separatism can be avoided. One is through a formal system of meetings and committees where staff from different departments come together. Similarly, interdepartmental project teams and 'task forces' can be set up to tackle particular initiatives and programmes. A third, less formal, strategy is that of individual managers 'networking' across the organisation; building up personal contacts in a number of departments.

A further way of providing integration-and also an important element of professional development for the individual job-holder-is by creating a 'matrix' structure. This gives individuals a 'line' management function-for example responsibility for a particular service point-and also membership of a 'team': for example, the team of librarians charged with providing service within a particular geographic area. The job description will give an indication of the relative proportion of time to be spent in each role (say, 60% line management, 40% team membership). A more sophisticated matrix may link the individual librarian to a particular territory (area team), a specific service (for example, children's services of reference work), and a section of stock (such as adult fiction). In this structure, the day-to-day administration of service points is likely to be delegated to Senior Library Assistants, thus creating an element of career progression for non-professional staff. One value of 'team librarianship' as developed in public libraries is that it can help to break down barriers of department separatism; as well as offering a cost-efficient means of deploying professional staff.

A number of other 'teams' will exist within the organisation to contribute to the process of integration/coordination and to the process of planning and forward development. There will be a Management Team of senior staff. There will also be various 'expert' teams bringing together staff with a particular area of expertise; for example, a team responsible for developing staff training programmes or for a particular area of service delivery-children's services, online searching, etc. In addition to these permanent or long-term teams, there will be teams brought together for a relatively short time to plan a particular project or deal with a specific task; for example, the implementation of an automated circulation control system. As well as breaking down departmental separatism by bringing together staff from different sections in order to tackle a common objective, these teams also bring an element of flexibility and innovation into the organisation's bureaucratic framework.

The concept of bureaucracy tends to get a bad press because of an association with complex regulations and procedures ('red tape') which tends to stifle initiative and promote inertia. But bureaucracy has positive values, in that it instills rationality and continuity into an organisation. Bureaucracy is expressed through:

- specification; structure shaped by job functions, not by particular individuals.
- stratification; hierarchy providing defined levels of authority.
- systems; of rules and procedures.

As well as an element of stability and consistency, the

bureaucratic approach also leads to impersonality-and thus to fairness and equality of treatment. Bureaucracy can be a safeguard against arbitrary and over-personalised dealing and decision-making. However, bureaucracy can lead to an overemphasis on rules, procedures and conformity.

There are two strategies which can help to inject a capacity for innovation and adaptation into the necessary bureaucratic framework. One is the use of short-term teams. The other is described by E.F. Schumacher as the fundamental task of achieving 'smallness' within an organisation.

'Smallness' is designed to avoid the problems normally associated with large organisations:

- remoteness and lack of commitment; an individual's feelings of personal responsibility for the success of the organisation diminish as the organisation grows.
- disaffection arising from the feeling of being 'just a cog in the machine'.
- 'red tape', inflexibility, delay, inertia (i.e. bureaucracy).

In terms of organisational structure, 'smallness' is achieved by decentralising the organisation into a number of small, relatively autonomous units. Library organisations are usually decentralised in structure-into a number of relatively small departments or branches-although management tends to remain centralised so that these small units have little real autonomy.

A particular value of 'smallness and the use of teams is the sense of 'team spirit' than can be generated. Group dynamics and the generation of team spirit emphasise the important of seeing an organisation's structure as a social system as well as a technical system. Bureaucracy and the organisation chart may be impersonal, but the success of an organisation-the quality of library service-depends on people.

There is a link between changing patterns of service provision and changing organisational structure. But structure alone does not determine the nature and quality of service. In order to bring in the 'people' dimension, considerations of structure need to be supplemented by the concept of organisational 'culture'.

The 'hidden' organisation and the concept of 'culture'

The concept of organisational 'culture' is difficult to describe with precision because, unlike structure, it cannot be codified into a series of organisation charts, a cycle of meetings, or a manual of procedures-although part of it can sometimes be captured in an organisation's mission statement or set of core values. 'Culture' has already been mentioned a number of times in this book:

- the impact on management thinking of the 'enterprise culture' vigorously promoted in the UK by the present government.
- the development of an organisational 'culture' which puts the customer first.
- the need, in an adaptive organisation, for a 'culture' which stimulates innovation, supports individual initiative, and accepts risk-taking; and which gives a 'bottom up' as well as a 'top down' dynamic to communications and decision-making.
- the 'loose-tight' concept of individual autonomy and selfcontrol within the framework of a strong

corporate 'culture' which constantly reinforces a few key values.

These examples suggest that culture is, at bottom, attitudinal. It is a set of attitudes-feelings, beliefs, values-which shape, and are reinforced by, actions. It is thus at the heart of the organisation's social system.

In all organisations the formal structure co-exists with an informal, 'hidden' set of dynamics. One example has already been seen: the informal but influential 'politicking' based on the 'King's Parade', which co-exists with the formal decision-making structure. One aspect of the 'hidden' organisation, then, is the informal power structure of influence which co-exists with the formal power structure of authority.

Traditionally, this 'hidden' organisation has been developed and reinforced through the social relationships which evolve within peer groups; and through the history and heritage-the corporate memory-of an organisation. It finds expression in the emergence of 'cliques' (tight knots of people who commune closely together, often to the exclusion of colleagues), the existence of an informal communications 'grapevine', and the establishment of 'unwritten rules'. These are an important guide to the workings and attitudes of the 'hidden' organisation and cover issues such as

- who to approach for information or advice on a particular issue.
- how to communicate with colleagues; when to write, or phone, or go to see someone.
- how to address colleagues; first names, or a more formal approach.

- dress codes; shirt sleeves? ties (properly tied, or loosened?)? jeans? skirts or trousers? etc.
- at work early or late; a sign of diligence-or inefficiency?

These 'hidden' dynamics are a powerful force in socialising individuals into the 'norms'-the accepted attitudes and behaviour-of the organisation.

This 'hidden' organisation has considerable value. It provides peer group support, extends communication networks, and so can assist with the smooth operation of the organisation. Rosemary Stewart suggests that it can even be responsible for the continued existence of organisations which would otherwise have collapsed; people develop informal methods of coping when organisations fail to adapt, formally, to changed circumstances.

The 'hidden' organisation, because it is based on social relationships, is naturally organic and adaptive. What is important, from the management perspective, is that these 'hidden' dynamics do not get out of line with the formal structure and objectives of the organisation. A successful-and happy-organisation is a single community where formal mechanisms and informal, 'hidden' dynamics work in harmony, mutually reinforcing each other. When this happens the organisation can be said to have evolved a healthy and coherent 'culture'.

Charles Handy's Understanding organisations, which focusses on the 'psychology' of organisations and the people who work in them, offers a useful typology of organisational cultures.

The power culture is entrepreneurial and competitive. There is little bureaucracy and much individual autonomy. Communication is verbal, decision-making is a highly 'political' process based on the power of individual personalities. People are judged on results. This is thrusting and dynamic culture which can work well in small organisations and at a time of rapid change. However, size can be a problem. Handy uses the image of a web to portray this culture-and the web can break if it gets too big or tries to link together too many activities.

The role culture suits large organisations operating in a stable environment. Power is based on position in the formal hierarchy. There is a clear structure of departmental responsibilities and bureaucratic procedures. It is important that individuals follow the correct process. This culture offers security and predictability, but change in the external environment can be a problem. Handy's image is of a Greek temple-and the foundations become insecure when the ground shakes.

Task culture is focussed on getting the job done. People and resources are brought together into project groups or task forces to 'get on with it'. Within the group power is based on expertise. Handy's image is of a net or network. This culture is good where flexibility, adaptability and responsiveness are needed. However it does not lend itself to control/coordination or to building strength in depth. It also needs an appropriately bountiful resource environment. When resources become limited, senior management has to control methods as well as results, and teams begin to compete, using political influence, for available resources. The task culture changes to a role or power culture.

This analysis of the resources environment's impact on organisational culture is particularly relevant to library service where, currently, there are often severe resource constraints. The task culture can provide the adaptability and innovation needed at a time of discontinuous change-hence the use of matrix structures and temporary teams within library organisations. But the need to allocate resources in a context of competing priorities shifts the emphasis to a role power culture. Decisions have to be taken which will be unpopular with some people. A current difficulty within library management is to reconcile these conflicting cultures.

Considerations of organisational culture have to take into account the 'psychological contract' between the individual and the organisation. This is the 'hidden' contract, based on expectations and motivation, which co-exists with the formal contract of employment.

> This psychological contract is essentially a set of expectations. The individual has a set of results that he expects from his organisation, results that will satisfy certain of his needs and in return for which he will expend some of his energies and talents. Similarly the organisation has its set of expectations of the individual and its list of payments or outcomes that it will give to him.

An important element in this 'contract' is affinity between the culture of the organisation and an individual's expectations and aspirations. An individual with a need for security will feel comfortable within a role culture. This might feel stifling to an individual with a need for recognition and 'self actualisation' (that is, 'stretching' oneself to realise one's full potential); that person might have the strength, confidence and ruthlessness to operate successfully in a power culture. On the other hand, and individual with a need for group affiliation or the expression of expertise might find the most suitable niche in a task culture.

When managing change and dealing with the restructuring of organisations, it is important to remember the interaction between organisational culture and individual psychology. A change in culture can have a profound effect on the 'psychological contract' which conditions the attitudes and behaviours of individuals within the organisation.

The person culture in which the structure or organisation only exists to serve the cluster of individuals within it. 'Barristers' chambers, architects partnerships, hippy communes, small consultancy practices, families and similar organisations can have this person orientation. In this culture, influence is shared and when power is exercised it is on the basis of expertise. Although there are few organisations where this culture predominates, there are many individuals whose personal preference is for this type of approach. 'Specialists in organisations-computer people in business organisations, consultants in hospitals, architects in city government-often feel little allegiance to the organisation but regard it rather as a place to do their thing with some accruing benefit to the main employer'.

This cast of mind is relevant to library service for two reasons. First, because of the increasing number of non-librarian specialists being employed within library organisations-people with expertise in systems, marketing, personnel, finance, administration, etc.-whose 'psychological contract' with the library may be shaped by this viewpoint. Second, because librarians themselves can think in this way. As specialists with a particular expertise their expectations and aspirations may well be framed in terms of 'the profession' rather than the organisation in which they find themselves currently working. This is one possible reason for the barriers which can build up, in some libraries, between professional and non-professional staff. The latter think of their work in relation to the organisation and, ideally, the customer community; and they sometimes perceive professional staff as being more interested in furthering their professional careers than in serving the needs of that library and its customers.

There are a number of factors which can determine the culture of an organisation:

- the size of the organisation;
- the age and history of the organisation;
- the organisation's purpose, objectives and activities;
- the resource environment within the organisation;
- external environments which form 'contingent factors' for the organisation;
- the people in the organisation; their expectations, aspirations and motivation.

From this list it is clear that there can often be a mix of different cultures within the same organisation. For example, the activities of a cataloguing department lend themselves to a culture-thoughtful and precise application of rules suggesting a role culture-different from that of a team of community librarians, where a strong focus on the team and the job suggests a task culture. The list also suggests that organisational cultures changes over time and through changing circumstances. Cultural change, however can be a slow and sometimes painful process, bound up as it is with the need for attitudes and behaviours to change.

To operate successfully within an organisation, a

manager needs to understand the dynamics of how that organisation works. Those dynamics are based not just on the formal structure but also on the 'hidden' organisation which co-exists with it. Structures are made up of people, and the manager needs to be aware of the psycho-dynamics of individuals, interpersonal relations, and groups. It is this psychological dimensions which drives the attitudes and values underpinning the concept of organisational culture.

- The manager as coach, not just devising plans, but motivating people by careful and detailed attention to them as individuals.
- The manager as value-shaper, reiterating and reinforcing the core values of the organisation by speech and action.
- The need for managers to 'walk the talk'; to show integrity and consistency-practise what they preach-in order to shape values and motivate individuals.
- The need for managers to get around the workplace, visibly and approachably. The Excellent books all stress the value of MBWA (Managing By Wandering Around). In addition this 'wandering around'—in the customer community as well as within the organisation itself-keeps a manager in close touch with current situations and information to which the organisation may have to respond or adapt.
- The importance of 'small stuff-the succession of brief encounters that characterise the manager's day of, in Mintzberg's phrase, 'brevity, variety and fragmentation'.

Making the best use of these brief encounters is the

fundamental message of The one minute manager by Blanchard and Johnson which stresses the importance of brief ('one minute') but effective sessions of goal-setting, praising, and reprimand.

Books like the Excellence sequence and The one minute manager are sometimes dismissed as 'pop' management. In fact, they present-in clear and often vibrant language-fundamental insights into the dynamics of organisations and the psychology of individuals at work. The three issues on which The one minute manager focusses (goal-setting, praising, reprimand) are, for example, core elements in the process of 'developing people' which Peter Drucker sees as an essential part of a manager's job.

In search of excellence and The winning streak both offer a checklist of the key attributes of 'excellent' organisations. Although these attributes appear in different sequences, are expressed in different terminologies, and refer to different nations, there is considerable consensus regarding the characteristics of successful organisations. What follows is a synthesis of those attributes, arranged under four main headings

- Purpose
  - clear sense of the fundamentals of the business
  - clear objectives
  - no dilution by diversification
- Market orientation
  - continuous market research
  - feedback from customers
  - care for quality control and customer service

- integrity in dealing with customers
- care to develop a good public image

• Organisation

- structure
  - kept simple
  - few staff at headquarters: most out 'in the field'
  - decentralised, with delegated authority and considerable autonomy
- control
  - concern for the planning process
  - clear objectives, with feedback on results
  - constant reinforcement of core values
- culture
  - 'hands on' involvement by mangers: to transmit core values, and to generate commitment, enthusiasm and pride
  - attitude supportive of innovation and entrepreneurship: a positive attitude to risk-taking (with tolerance of mistakes as part of the learning process); a bias for action and experimentation-try it out, get it done.

• People

- productivity through people
  - respect for the individual
  - care for the motivation and morale of individuals

- recognition that 'rank and file' staff are the root source of efficiency and quality of service

- leadership
    - visible management (e.g. MBWA)
    - creation of an environment which encourage the exercise of leadership at all levels of management.

This checklist provides a useful summary of the key issues raised in this book so far. It also illustrates how much organisational dynamics are intertwined with the psychology of people. Implicit throughout the checklist, for example, is the connection between excellent organisational performance and good interpersonal communications.

The importance of communication

The Excellence literature illustrates the link between communications and organisational performance. The one minute manager shows the link between communications and effective management. In these books, the focus tends to be on management communication which is *ad hoc* and verbal. Every organisation will also contain two other types of communication: the formal communications structure, usually of meetings and memoranda; and the informal 'grapevine'. It is important for managers to realise that, however much an organisation becomes a single community, there will always be a network of communication and social relationships from which management is excluded.

Ken Jones suggests that these informal communications networks play a vital role in easing the 'psycho-social strain' which individuals can experience in a bureaucratic organisation. They do this in three ways:

- as a socialising force, giving people a sense of 'belonging', of being a member of the group with whom they communicate.
- as a part of the 'politicking' process, enabling people to attempt to influence the decision-making process.
- as an information network, transmitting news more rapidly than the 'official channels'.

The informal 'grapevine' is also, of course, one of the key ways in which an organisation's culture is developed and reinforced. Stories circulate through the grapevine and then become part of the 'oral history' of the organisation to be reiterated from time to time. These will inevitably focus on an individual or an event in a way which promoted certain values and attitudes.

Formal communications usually exist on paper. The written document provides a record and tends to be worded more precisely than a verbal interchange. Of course, simply writing and sending a message is no indication that the message has been received or understood or acted on. There is no (immediate) feedback. However, much communication in organisations tends to be of this one-way, paper-based type-memos, reports, bulletins of 'routine instructions' to all staff.

Meetings form the other major element of formal communication-regular committees, or specially convened meetings. There may well be considerable verbal interaction at these meetings, but the official record of discussions and decisions will be the 'minutes', a document written up afterwards and formally approved at the next meetings. Discussion will also have been largely limited to those items included on a preset 'agenda' of issues for consideration.

This formal, bureaucratic process is important-it provides a stable, impersonal and regular means by which issues can be raised and decisions made. But it is likely to be somewhat slow and ponderous. The vast majority of useful communications will take place around these meetings, rather than in them.

Communications within an organisation can be described in terms of four directions:

— downward, following the hierarchical chain of command.

— upward, through a variety of mechanisms; reporting systems designed to monitor performance; participative planning and decision-making structures; the machinery of consultation and negotiation with trade union representatives.

— horizontally across, between peers in the same work groups, or departments and individuals on the same level of the hierarchy.

— diagonally across, for example, when a department in one part of the organisation needs the assistance of a senior specialist from another section.

In each direction there can be barriers to good communication. Within the hierarchy the quality of communication can diminish as it filters down-or up-through the chain of command. The desire to spread only good news gets in the way of full and accurate upward communication; information is 'laundered' as it passes higher up the hierarchy. A sense of status and of 'only telling people what they need to know' can obstruct the flow of information downward. This can lead to what has been described as the 'mushroom management' syndrome-people are kept in the dark and occasionally get a pile of fertiliser (or something similar) dumped on them.

In libraries, the split between professional and non-professional staff can lead to breakdowns in communication based on hierarchy. Non-professional staff are rarely included in the organisation's cycle of formal meetings and are heavily dependent on their line manager-often a relatively recently qualified professional i a junior management position-in order to feel included in the communications network.

Barriers to communication across the organisation can include geographic dispersal and the compartmentalism of different departments and specialisms. Library organisations can have particular difficulties here. Library organisations are often geographically dispersed with a lack of communication between 'central' and the branches in public library systems; or between the 'main library' and the site libraries in some academic institutions. There is also sometimes a lack of communication between functional departments (lending, reference, bibliographic services, etc.)

Technology may well be able to help in breaking down some of these cross-organisational barriers. Electronic mail is a valuable hybrid which can have (like verbal communication) an interactive element and which can be (like written communication) precisely worded and formally recorded. Email networks enable staff to communicate frequently irrespective of geographic dispersal. A number of the 'integrated systems' (automating cataloguing, circulation control, acquisitions, serials control, etc.) in use in large UK libraries have the capability to support an Email network. It may be that Email will become a useful tool by which management can widen communication flow and increase participation in discussions and decisions within library organisations. Good communications are essential to a healthy organisation and a contented workforce. As Anne Mathews emphasises 'high morale and motivation stem from open communications'.

There are a number of things which can be done-aside from exploring the potential of new technology-if managers wish to increase the effectiveness of organisational communications. One is simply for management to be aware of the need to review communications. The concept of the 'open door' (as in 'if you want to come and see me, my door is always open') illustrates the discrepancy which often exists between a manager's self perception and the way in which that manager's style is perceived by other members of staff. The manager may think the door is open-but in practice the manager is often out of the office, or busy, and staff may feel inhibited about just 'popping in for a chat'.

A second strategy is to create an environment which encourages communication. This involves managers taking pains to listen more effectively-too often, meetings become a series of monologues rather than a dialogue or true discussion. It also involves creating a climate of trust. Staff will not offer their observations, opinions or information if that material is then used to exploit a situation, condemn an action, or gossip about an individual.

The third strategy is to create 'communication opportunities' within the organisation. The use of temporary teams and matrix structures is valuable in this regard, as is a culture which supports the concept of 'management by wandering about'. Coffee (or tea) breaks and lunchtimes are also excellent opportunities for informal communications, as is the time-honoured tradition of 'a quick drink after work'. Some managers also see social events-Christmas parties, summer barbeques, charity sports events, etc.-as an important part of this process and act as a catalyst for such events.

Social events bring people together and can build a feeling of collective identity and 'team spirit'. They can help to break down barriers of status and formality and so can contribute to better interpersonal relations. They bring people out of their departments and into the organisation as a whole thus encouraging integration and a sense of overall purpose. Above all, they can take people out of their job-roles and enable them to 'be themselves' as human beings.

Of course, this can be dangerous. The stereotype is of the 'office party', fuelled by alcohol and spiced with romance, which leads to embarrassment or calamity. When people are taken out of their usual roles the results are unpredictable. There may be people-particularly those who subscribe to a 'role' culture- who feel uncomfortable or out-of-place at such events, or who chose not to attend and then feel 'left out' of the group. But the potential for positive outcomes, in terms of team-building and networking, can outweigh the possibilities for discomfort or disaster.

An organisation is a community, a mix of the mechanistic and the human, of technical and social systems. formal structures co-exist with the 'hidden' organisation of unwritten rules and alliances. Explicit contracts of employment co-exist with the implicit 'psychological contract' between each individual and the organisation. Feelings, beliefs and shared values form the 'culture' which shapes attitudes and behaviour. This 'soft stuff of people and their motivations is a key factor in determining the 'hard facts' of organisational performance. All are linked by formal and informal networks of communication.

Charles Handy writes of management style in terms of 'structuring' and 'supporting'. Clearly, managers need to give attention to both functions-and good communications are central to both. It is important to review organisational structures, bureaucratic processes, and formal channels of communication. It is equally important to be alive to the 'hidden' dimensions of individual psychology, organisational culture, and social networks. To promote a sense of community and nurture the social systems within the organisation, it makes sense to provide opportunities for informal socialising outside the roles and restrictions of the organisation itself.

3

General Office Functions

Each organisation performs certain office functions for implementing various decisions taken by the management from time to time. A library also performs similar functions, though in a modified forms due to its special functions and jobs. These office functions fall under the following categories:

1. Committee work.
2. Personnel administration and coordination.
3. Finance and Accounts.
4. Publicity.
5. Binding.
6. Building and equipment.
7. Correspondence work.
8. Stores, stationery and Printing.
9. Maintenance of Library Records.
10. Preparation and Publication of Annual Reports.
11. Maintenance of Library Statistics.
12. Conducting Library Surveys.

Correspondence work

The correspondence work consists of the following distinct jobs:

1. Inward correspondence/Receipt of Mail.
2. Replying the letters/Fresh Correspondence.
3. Outward correspondence/despatch of Mail.
4. Filing work.

Inward correspondence

A library gets the following types of letters etc. through either mail, chief mail or urgent mail, and by hand from various sources:-

1. Readers' letters containing suggestions for book selection, applications for admission to the library, remittance of fines, refund of cash deposits etc., requests and suggestions for improvement of library services, reservation of reading materials etc.
2. Book lists and catalogues from publishers.
3. Indents from members of the Book Selection Committee/Heads of Departments.
4. Bills and Receipts from book suppliers.
5. Correspondence dealing with other sections of the library.
6. Misdelivered mail.

The following routines are involved in dealing with the inward correspondence;-

1. Receipt of the whole correspondence by the Librarian.
2. Sorting and classification of correspondence.
3. Registering in the Inward Correspondence Register and stamping and noting the Receipt No. and date.

4. Posting of the number and date of receipt of reply against appropriate items in the concerned Outwards Correspondence Register.
5. Transmitting the correspondence to various sections of the library after entering it in an appropriate diary and obtaining and verifying the signatures of the concerned person of the section.
6. Preparing the list of inward correspondence in arrears.
7. Disposing of the misdelivered correspondence by transmitting to proper quarters.

Replaying correspondence/Fresh correspondence

Each section takes steps for disposing of the correspondence. The following jobs are involved:-

1. Drafting the reply.
2. Getting it approved from the Section Incharge/ Librarian.
3. Getting fair copies typed/written in hand and comparing these with the original letters.
4. Drafting, stencil cutting and duplicating circular draft letters.
5. Filing the stencils and cleaning the Duplicator.
6. Preparing copies of lists of books and other items.
7. Sending the correspondence to the Librarian for his signatures and transmitting it to Outward Correspondence Section.

Outward correspondence/despatch of mail

In the outward correspondence section, the following routines are involved:

1. Storing, classifying, arranging and signature

verifying of the outward correspondence received from various sections of the library.

2. Entering the particulars of each letter etc. in the appropriate Outward Correspondence Register and assigning concerned despatch number and date on the copies of each letter despatched.

3. Preparing an envelope for each letter and writing full address of the addressee on it.

4. Closing each envelope, weighing it and affixing postage stamps of appropriate value on each of the despatched letters and posting them against each item.
(The letters which are to be delivered by hand through a messenger to the local offices or persons are not stamped.)

5. Sending the mail to the post office and other offices through messengers asking them to deliver the letters and obtain necessary acknowledgments.

6. Verifying the acknowledgements.

7. Posting the number and date of each letter despatched against the concerned item in the Inward Correspondence Register.

8. Preparing the stamp account and posting it in the Postage Stamps Register.

9. If the stamps are likely to be exhausted, an order for the supply of stamps is prepared and sent through the office accountant.

10. Receiving the supply of stamps and accounting it in the Stamps Register and storing the stamps in the Stamps Chest.

11. Sending the office copies of the despatched letters to the concerned sections for filing in the respective files.

Filing work

1. Each section receives back the copies of the despatched letter.
2. Each such copy is filed in the concerned file.

Stores, stationery and printing

Stores Section is concerned with the acquiring, storing and distributing of all store and stationery articles required in a library. Besides the store and stock articles required in a modern office, the following articles should specially be kept in store:-

1. Forms and Registers as required by various sections of the library.
2. Catalogue Blank Cards.
3. Binding Materials.

Acquisition of stores

Except some stray articles, which may be acquired occasionally from the pretty cash account, the supplies of stores should be acquired annually on sanctioned and competitive rates from approved firms either by the parent body or by the library itself by calling quotations for the supply of requisite store articles, forms and registers. The quantum of supplies should be based on the following:-

1. The Maximum to which stock should be bought up periodically-say, once in a year.
2. The minimum below which the stock should not go i.e. when the stock reaches that figures, steps should be taken for replenishment.
3. The annual consumption.
4. The quantum of issue.

This work involves the following distinct jobs:

1. Asking various sections of the library to send their store requirements for the coming years.
2. Preparing the rough indents after taking into account the consumption of articles in the previous year for each section.
3. Preparing a final indent after consulting the Librarian. Care is to be taken that the cost of the indented articles is not more than the budgeted amount for the purpose.
4. Sending indent to the parent body/central executive for acquisition of store articles.
5. Receiving the bills from the suppliers; passing them after necessary verification; certification; transmitting the bill to the Accounts section for payments; and noting down Voucher Numbers in the Stock and Store Register.

Storing and housing of articles

After the supplies are received from the suppliers or the parent body/central executives, these are to be stored in a classified order according to the numbers allotted to each of the articles. These are to be kept in appropriate cartons, tins or other containers so that these are not spoiled by rain, dust, dirt or vermin. The Store Room should be kept scrupulously clean and tidy. If the Quantum Principle of distribution is adopted, and if the articles themselves are packed in quanta, the tidiness of the storing arrangement will be secured. Further, the quarterly verification of the Stock will be greatly facilitated.

4

LIBRARY ADMINISTRATION FUNCTIONS

Library is a social institution charged with the most enviable function of dispensing knowledge to the ignorant and the informed alike. 'Vidya-dan' i.e. imparting of knowledge has been considered as the most sacred task in Ancient India and Manu rightly allotted this job to the most gifted persons of the society of that age. The Brahmins were at the uppermost rung of the ladder and so they were made responsible for performing the task of impacting knowledge. Libraries of Vidya Bhandaras being indispensable, had a pride of place in society. The administration of such an important social institution naturally demands greater attention that given in the past.

The main function of a library is the collection and preservation of knowledge for its dissemination to all. Its conservation for posterity is also an important duty of a library. The libraries have changed the outmoded concept of preserving a large number of reading materials for the sake of preservation only. Gurudeva Tagore rightly remarked, "the extent to use to which the reading material of a library is put, should determine its importance rather than the staggering number of volumes". He deprecated the idea of putting more emphasis on collecting books alone. He gave an example of a millionaire. "He is judged great in a gathering, not by what he has but what he gives". He illustrated this point by bringing out the difference between a dictionary and literature. The former was a depository of words while the latter was a medium through which the words were used and developed. Gurudeva gave more importance to literature. Similarly, Gurudeva pointedly remarked that constant and increased use of its books gave a library its significance.

All our efforts should, in fact, be channelised to fulfill these basic functions of a library and that can be achieved only if we plan and implement the decisions in the most scientific and economic way. The Five Laws of Library Science of Dr. Ranganathan provide requisite guidance on the subject.

Library Administration can be studied from theoretical as well as practical angles. To have better results, practical administration must be based on sound theoretical principles. On the other hand, to get sound theoretical principles, these should be based on practical experiences.

A library presents almost the same problems as are encountered with in any other social institution-a school, a college, or a commercial or industrial undertaking. It would, therefore, be appropriate to take into account the administrative functions of other social institutions and to apply them to libraries with necessary modifications.

Definition and functions of administration

An organisation, business or enterprise is established with an aim to achieve a set goal. How to achieve it? Who has to achieve it? An organisational structure is raised, an administrative machinery is created and a management authority is appointed. The administrative machinery is responsible for laying down the basic policies of the organisation, for providing a suitable organisational structure to achieve the set aims of the organisation and for appointing the management personnel for translating into reality the desired aims. "That phase of a business enterprise which concerns itself with the overall determination of the major policies and objectives is Administration. For the administrative functions to be effective in operations a 'doing' function is required. Management is the executive function that concerns itself with the carrying out of the administrative policy laid down by Administration. It directs the active operations within the enterprise and combines the work of the employees with the available capital, equipment and materials to produce an acceptable product. It also markets the product or service according to the broad policies established by Administration.

Similar views have been expressed by other authorities. J. William Schulze considered 'Administration' as "the force which lays down the object for which an organisation and its management are to strike and the broad policies under which they are to operate". According to him, 'Management' is "the force which leads, guides and directs an organisation in the accomplishment of pre-determined object." There is a confusion between the terms 'Administration' and 'Management". Sometimes these are inter-changeable. But at others, one is considered a generic term while the other a specie. "Administration is that function of management which actually executes or carries out the objectives for which the enterprise is organised. This function initiates the work to be performed, sees that personnel is fitted to the task and trained to operate properly, and in general cases for everyday routine necessary to ensure that men, materials and equipments are functioning properly towards the desired end".

Henri Fayol, who was a successful French industrialist wrote his famous treatise "General and Industrial Administration". He based it on his rich and long experience as an administrator. According to him, the operations which occur in a business can be divided into six main groups-technical, commercial, financial, security, accounting and managerial. He regarded `administration' as one of these six major functions.

"Administration," he said, "regarded in this way must not be confused with government. To govern is to conduct an undertaking towards its objective by seeking to make the best possible use of all the resources at its disposal; it is, in fact, to ensure the smooth working of the six essential functions. Administration is only one of these functions...."

Functions of administration

Fayol brought out five distinguishing functions of administration, namely, to plan, to organise, to command, to co-ordinate, and to control. The words 'To plan' use for the original word 'prevoyance' means 'to forecast, and 'to plan'. Each of these six functions of administration can be grouped into two groups i.e. process and effect. Accordingly, 'Forecasting, leads to 'planning', 'organisation' is for ensuring 'co-ordination' and 'command' provides 'control'. Fayol's analysis of administrative functions can be implied as under from his list of 'Administrative Duties'.

1. Investigation→Forecasting→Planning.
2. Appropriateness→Organisation→Co-ordination.
3. Order→Command→Control.

Luther Gulick adopted Fayol's ideas and restated the functions under the catchword 'PODSCORB'. It stands for the following seven functions:-

1. Planning.
2. Organising.
3. Staffing.
4. Directing.
5. Co-ordinating.
6. Reporting.
7. Budgeting.

Planning

The first function of an administrator is to plan and forecast i.e. determining the goals and ideals of an institution. The ways and means to achieve these objectives are thought out on a plenary basis. These outlines are given concrete shape and a regular framework of authority is established in such a manner that maximum work of best quality is ensured at a minimum cost with minimum efforts. Planning presupposes the stock-taking of the existing conditions and the relevant causes. The solutions are suggested for removing the defects by phased systematic programme. The economic planning is concerned with the production of maximum output with minimum input. In planning, entire wastage is avoided and every constituent factor is made to contribute its own share.. The efforts are made to remove the basic defects and their future implications are taken care of. In library planning, the locality, its make-up as regards its physical features, its linguistic divisions, its cultural diversities a services. The pros and cons are properly studied so that the service is effective and long enduring.

Organising

Planning to be fruitful needs a sound organisation, which means that such a structure of authority is established which is capable to achieving the set goals. Through this structure, work subdivisions are arranged, defined and co-ordinated for the set goal. This structure is needed to bring together all the staff members in such a scientific way that the work is done most efficiently and smoothly. In library organisation, the decisions is taken as to what kind of authority is to be provided for an area of service. Should the authority be autonomous or part and parcel of the Local Government machinery? If it is to be autonomous of the Local Government Authority, it is to be found out as to whether this autonomous body would be capable of raising and collecting enough finances for running the library.

Staffing

An organisation for its efficient working is totally dependent upon proper staffing and recruiting policies. The staff employed should have special aptitudes and capabilities for performing a particular kind of job. For example, the Chief Librarian of a public library should be sympathetic towards readers and should be capable of understanding the varied tastes of the public. Besides advanced learning, he should be able to command respect by his qualities of leadership. He should be a competent person to serve as a Public Relations Office i.e. to serve as a liaison officer between the readers and the books. The common people consider him a guide and the librarian should come up to their expectations.

A University Librarian, in addition, should have an aptitude for research if he wants to become a successful librarian. He must have a sound grounding in research methodology. The other junior staff members should be appointed keeping in view their aptitude for various jobs. The practical experience of various jobs at the credit of applicants for various posts should be taken into consideration at the time of their appointment. 'Staffing' includes the training of staff and the maintenance of favourable conditions of work for them.

Directing

The harmony and efficiency of the staff depends upon the personal qualities of the Chief Librarian. He should be capable of performing his duties as a leader. It implies that besides possessing knowledge, he should be able to infuse confidence amongst the staff members. He should be able to boost up their morale. He should be an example to be followed by his subordinates. In other words, he should not be frustrated with his job. Rather, he should do his job with zeal. He should be ready to sacrifice his personal comforts for the sake of library work and library staff. He should prove an ideal leader by dint of his hard work and sincerity for the staff welfare. 'Directing' includes continuous decision making and embodying them in general and specific orders and instructions.

Co-ordinating

Leadership will be successful only if the leader can properly inter-relate various parts of an organisation in a harmonious way. This co-ordination can be achieved if the head knows well all the jobs and effects such an automatic administrative machinery that he feels practically no necessity to interfere. It depends upon the kind of organisation which has been brought into being i.e. as to whether he introduces Line Type or Line and Staff Type of structure or Functional Type of organisation. In other words, there should be delegation of powers but staff members in whom the powers are vested should also be made responsible for their jobs. They should be answerable to the Chief. An automatic apparatus should be effected by means of introducing a practice of getting periodical reports from the various Section Heads. He should allow these Heads to use their initiative but whenever there is some difficulty or misunderstanding, the Chief should thrash out the problem in periodical staff meetings.

Reporting

Reporting' means keeping authorities, to whom the executive head of an organisation is responsible, informed about the progress or regress of his work. To perform this duty efficiently, the executive head has to keep himself and his subordinates informed about their jobs and performances through research, records and inspection. It is a sound principle or organisation that a periodical report is asked from a head of an enterprise. Such a report should be factual one based upon actual and faithful statistical data. The Chief of a library has to submit an annual report to the executive authority concerned. This practice keeps the Chief vigilant about his own activities since he knows that somebody else above him is keeping a watch upon him. Laski, a renowned political philosopher, observed, "vigilance is the price of freedom". The Chief Librarian, in turn, has to ask various Section Heads of his library to maintain proper records and statistics of the work performed by their respective subordinates so that a faithful and factual report is presented to the former.

Budgeting

'Budgeting' includes fiscal planning, accounting and control. No organisation can function properly without adequate finances. But it is difficult to obtain enough funds for all kinds of organisations, especially libraries, which are dependent and spending bodies. Libraries do not earn any revenues in the physical sense. Their services, though essential for the well-being of the individual, the society and the government, are not considered apparently indispensable. Consequently, the legislators and bureaucrats alike reject the demands of libraries on one or the other pretext. The libraries have been given almost the lowest priority in matter of allocation of funds. So the librarian has to muster strength and acquire necessary skill and tact for securing adequate funds. He has to convince the authorities about the usefulness of the service rendered by libraries. This can be achieved only if he advances tangible and plausible reasons for each of his demands. The authorities can be convinced easily by statistical data. So the librarian should maintain proper statistics of income and expenditure of his library. He should ensure proper utilisation of fiscal grants without any avoidable wastage.

In addition to the above-mentioned functions, the following two functions are considered essential for an efficient administration:-

Control

The Chief or the Supervisor will have to be ever vigilant about the rate of progress of the work. He has to ensure best quality and maximum quantity of work from his workers. In order to achieve this the Chief has to control effectively his subordinates. He has to inspect their work personally. He has to keep an eye upon the methods of performing specific jobs assigned to individual workers, the end products and overall costs of production/services.

Motivation

The Chief can achieve his aim of maximum production

only if he instils enthusiasm and team-work amongst his workers. Unless the workers perform their jobs willingly and conscientiously, the aim cannot be achieved. The workers must be motivated by providing congenial service conditions and environments. They must be made to realise that if they work more, they will get rewards for the same.

Principles of library administration

A library is a social institution. Every constituent of the society wants the library of flourish. On the other hand, the library is a part and parcel of the social framework. It is for the society. Without the society, the library will become extinct. It, in order to flourish, must not lose sight of the principles followed in administering other social institutions both private and public. Miles and Martin state, "The fundamental point is that the librarian is a public administrator. The library is an integral part of vast public service system, a circumstance that is most evident in the field of financial support. And in accomplishing his purpose the librarian performs administrative operations essentially similar to those of other public agencies..Two supplementary assumptions form the basis of the relationship of the library to the general theory of management and to the more specific principles of public administration. The first is that the management of a library involves functions that are essentially similar to those found in any co-operative enterprise..the second assumption is that fundamental tenets of public administration-as to managerial structure and fiscal organisation, for example-apply to such agencies as the school, the police department, and the public library".

The aim of a library is to ensure maximum use of its reading materials by maximum number of persons of its public. This is to be achieved by minimum output at most economical terms. This involves the application of principles of business administration. The purpose of a business organisation is to secure maximum profit. This is achieved by its at the most economical rates with minimum input. So basically, a library and a business organisation are measured in monetary terms while those of a library are judged from the utilisation of library funds for providing maximum reading services to its clientele. It is like other 'service' organisations e.g. Education Services.

A librarian, besides, being a scholar, should also understand the basic principles of business management. He should be a manager of an enterprise and should have adequate administrative acumen. The following basic principles, though pertaining to business management, can be applied to library administration with minor modifications and adjustments taking into account the aims and goals of a library.

Unity of command and management

The first pre-requisite of a good organisation is the Unity of Command-investing one person with all powers so far as his particular sphere of working is concerned. Dispersal of powers and functions to a group of people makes nobody responsible. Joint responsibility is nobody's responsibility. It is essential to have consistency in decisions and their proper implementation otherwise one person may interpret the decisions in one direction whereas the other person may take it in quite an opposite manner. It will create unnecessary confusion both within the group of administrators and their subordinates. The unity of command ensures efficiency and quick decisions. Each worker knows as to from whom he has to take orders and to whom he has to give orders. Ultimately, everybody is responsible to one executive head.

This principle of "unity of command" can be implemented by providing for "unit of management' which implies that the staff members work in a proper set-up and atmosphere which can be possible only if there is unity in planning and its implementation devices. All planning should lead to the fulfillment of the common goal of the library and all the individual ideas should be subordinated to the achievement of the main aim.

Scalar chain

"There must be a clear line of formal authority running from the top to the bottom of every organisation". To get work from other persons is difficult than doing a particular job by oneself, and it is especially so where scores and hundreds of people are engaged in a particular pursuit. For this purpose, a right type of organisational structure is essential. A choice is to be made out of the following structures which have been in constant use in various types of organisations and enterprises. But a proper selection would be possible only if these types of organisational set-ups are discussed at some length.

Line type

When all the workers are responsible direct to the head of the section/institution and to nobody else, the institution is said to have a line type of organisation. In bigger institutions, the control by the Chief himself becomes somewhat physically difficult if not impossible and he delegates certain powers to his deputies/ assistants. These deputies/assistants are directly responsible to the head through an intermediary authority. Suppose, one library, besides other junior staff members, has got 5 Assistant Librarians, one Deputy Librarian and Librarian. In a line form of set-up, the Assistant Librarians will be responsible to the Deputy Librarian and not to the Librarian direct. This system implies a hierarchy of officers and it has got its merits and demerits. This rigid type of organisation is found in military organisations. This mechanism can be successful in very small libraries but it is liable to break down in larger institutions. The specimen of a Line type of organisation is given as under:-

(a) Public Library

Municipal Council/Local Library Authority

Library Board/Committee

Librarian

Deputy Librarian

Acquisition Sec. Asstt. Lib.	Classification Cat. Asstt. Lib.	Periodicals Sec. Asstt. Lib.	Ref. & Lending Sec. Asstt. Lib.	Evening Shift Incharge Asstt. Lib.
Library Asstt.	Library Asstt.	Library Asstt.	Library Asstt.	Library Asstt.
Junior Library Asstt.	Junior Library Asstt.	Junior Library Asstt.	Junior Library Asstt.	Junior Library Asstt.
Clerk	Clerk	Clerk	Janitor	Janitor
Peon	Peon	Peon	Peon	Peon

(a) University Library

Senate/Court
|
syndicate/Executive Council
|
Vice-Chancellor
|
Academic Council
|
Library Committee
|
Librarian
|
Deputy Librarians
|

Acquisition Section Asstt. Lib.	Technical Section Asstt. Lib.	Periodicals Section Asstt. Lib.	Reference & Lending Sec. Asstt. Lib.	Evening Shift Incharge Asstt. Lib.
Library Asstt.	Library Asstt.	Library Asstt.	Library Asstt.	Library Asstt.
Junior Library Asstt.	Junior Library Asstt.	Junior Library Asstt.	Junior Library Asstt.	Junior Library Asstt.
Clerk	Clerk	Clerk	Janitor	Janitor
Peon	Peon	Peon	Peon	Peon

Line and staff type

'Line' denotes authority whereas 'Staff' stands for advice and counsel. The Staff type of administrative organisation is supplementary to the Line type and it does not serve as an alternative to the later. "A staff officer is one 'who is leaned on' for thinking, seeing, planning, recommending and reporting or co-ordinating, in some special aspect, in contrast to the line officer whose job is to give work instructions and get things done". In order to get sound advice, the work is divided into various departmental divisions and persons with specialised knowledge are made incharge of such divisions. Here, authority and advice are combined, though the executive authority remains with the Line type authorities but the auxiliary services are left to the Staff organisational heads e.g. cataloguing and classification, etc. are given in the charge of divisional heads.

These staff officials, though, do not come into direct contact of the readers, yet, become instrumental in making the library service effective.

The theory of organisation has undergone a lot of change. 'Staff and line are co-ordinates, operating not in a hierarchical relation to staff over line, but on a horizontal plans of authority and responsibility under the Chief executives'.

Those tasks which are considered not to be executive are generally delegated to Staff officers. These jobs relate to the provision of information and guidance to library research workers. The type of organisation which is a mixture of the Line and Staff types of organisations is illustrated below:

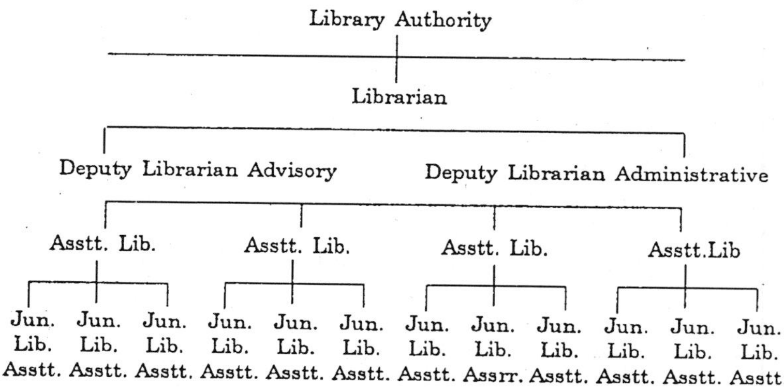

But in order to ensure proper functioning of these two kinds of organisations in one set-up, a proper co-ordination is essential. The necessity of co-ordination is felt because the Staff Officers being theoretical in their approach may make certain impracticable suggestions which may not be liked by the Line Officers and they may, on their part, reject these proposals prefunctorily. Consequently, there is a danger of an unnecessary conflict between the employees of an organisation.

Co-ordination is further essential because due to unmanageable size and complex procedures, every section remains engrossed in its own work and does not even try to know the work and workers of the other sections. Consequently, water-tight compart-mentalisation results. Co-ordination can be achieved by the Chief Librarian by calling frequent staff meetings and by appointing co-ordinators at various service points such as children, youth and adult departments.

Functional organisation

"Functional planning is found almost universally in nature". The line and Line Staff type of organisations create certain problems like lack of coordination amongst various sections. Even overlapping of duties is reported many times. It is thought advisable to define, once for all, the functions and duties of each person and it is done by dividing the whole library work by the type of jobs involved e.g. acquisition, classification, cataloguing, reference service and circulation etc. In this type of organisation, all the aspects of each particular job are but together under one Section Incharge respectively. For example, all the reading materials are acquired by the Incharge of Acquisition Section irrespective of the fact that the books relate to different subjects and languages. Similarly, the Incharge of Technical Section is responsible for the classification and cataloguing of all books irrespective of the fact that these belong to different subjects and languages. It is claimed that in this way, the functions of each person are clearly defined and over-lapping is almost completely eliminated and specialisation in particular jobs is secured.

The Chief Librarian and Deputy/Assistant Librarians are relieved from attending to the routine jobs. They are able to devote their time in planning future policies for the development of the library and in preparing programmes for closer relations between the staff, the readers and the books. "In most types of administration-and especially in library administration-the basis of planning likely to yield the best results is a functional basis, adopted to the needs of the particular administration.."

But this form of organisation is also not ideal. It becomes instrumental in widening the gulf between various departments and the persons working in each sections tend to forget all other technical jobs except that which comes to their lot. Secondly, under this form of organisation span of control increases. But these defects can be offset by introducing certain modifications. The first defect can be removed by holding frequent staff meetings and by shifting the duties of various assistants in rotation after every two years or so as has been put into practice by the author in the Himachal Pradesh University Library. The second defect can be offset by appointing one or two intermediary deputies/assistants who may be made responsible for particular departments.

Specimen of functional organisation of a university library

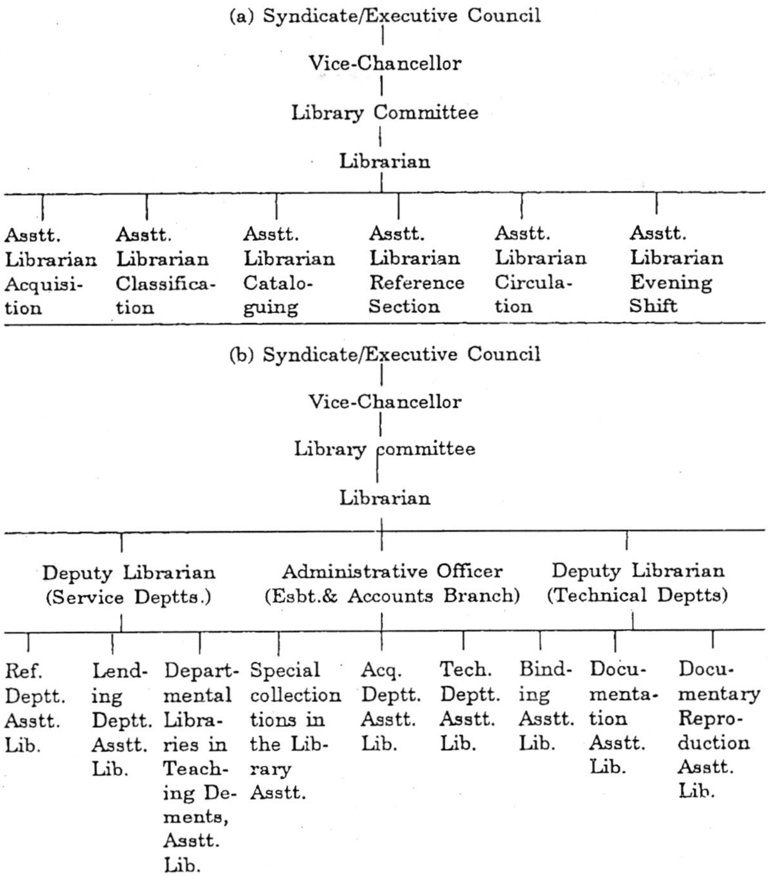

Arrangement by materials

Another arrangement followed in very large libraries is by materials. Special divisions are created for handling various kinds of materials. These are Books Division, Maps Division, Periodicals Division, Films Division, Government Publications Division, etc., etc. These division are responsible for acquisition, processing and making available the particular kinds of materials with which they deal. This kind of arrangement has got its own merits and demerits and can be usefully followed in libraries where these materials are received in large numbers. This kind of phenomenon is found in national and depository libraries. This arrangement is useful because each type of material is handled by specialists, proper treatment is ensured and wastage of time and energy of the staff is avoided. This system also avoids overlapping of duties and functions.

Subject arrangement

Since readers' approach is mainly by subject, they are becoming more and more conscious of their specific needs and this awakening on the part of the readers has put a heavy responsibility on the library staff. Unless they organise their collections in accordance with the approach of the readers, the library service may not be effective. In this type of organisational setup, library administrative machinery is geared up in such a manner that all work is divided on the basis of subjects. The general pattern is to divide the whole universe of knowledge into the following main groups:-

1. Humanities.
2. Social Sciences.
3. Biological Sciences.
4. Pure Sciences.

This system implies that one senior staff number is made incharge of each of these branches of knowledge. He is expected to be fully conversant with the subjects of his specialisation. It is better if he at least holds a Master's Degree in the concerned subject/subjects, because such a person should be able to answer many technical questions. It further implies that the Incharge of a Division will be responsible for the acquisition, preparation and servicing of the reading material of a particular subject field. The reference service is also done by the Divisional Head of a particular subject. The latest trend is towards the adoption of subject arrangement pattern and we find that many Universities in the United State of America and other countries of the world have adopted this type of organisation in their libraries. The universities of Cleveland, Los Angeles, Baltimore, and Rochester have got subject arrangement type of organisation in their libraries. This type of arrangement is very useful for the students and research scholars but it is more expensive than some other types of organisations.

Delegation of authority

In order to secure proper co-ordination and strategic leadership, authority is delegated. It implies that the Chief Executive surrenders some of his powers to his immediate subordinates. Thus he multiplies himself because his authority is manifested in many of his subordinates when they get his orders implemented. In this kind of decentralisation of authority, the Chief Executive rules by the principle of 'Administration by objectives' rather than by that of 'Administration by Authority'. In the former case, the Chief executive brings home the ideals and objectives of the organisation to his subordinates and secures their willing co-operation for fulfilling the set objectives. The responsibility devolves upon the subordinates. In the latter case, the orders are directly issued by the Chief Executive and all the subordinates are directly responsible to him and the work is got done by the show of authority and command.

There are always three jobs for top management:

(i) Managing the business as a whole;

(ii) Managing the managers (Subordinate executives); and

(iii) Managing the workers and the work to be done.

To ensure proper implementation of the abovementioned objectives the following essential elements must be provided:-

(i) Right type of leadership;

(ii) Clear understanding by every individual of the organisation as a whole, each section of it and the job assigned to every worker;

(iii) The delegation of powers should be commensurate with responsibility;

(iv) Decision making and their execution should be left to the subordinate heads so that they may gain confidence and may take initiative. In this way they would work with zeal;

(v) All the residual authority after defining the respective limits of the Chief Executive and subordinates should be left to the subordinate heads:

(vi) The decisions which are long range, multirelational, qualitative and complex, should generally be referred upward, and

(vii) The Chief Executive should keep a vigil and restraint upon the subordinate heads to ensure that the decisions taken by them are in conformity with the general policies laid down by the top management.

Departmentation

Proper job analysis and assignment of jobs should be planned in such a manner that no overlapping in duties occurs. This can be achieved by establishing various departments. The powers, functions and duties of various departmental heads must be clearly defined. Like jobs should be put under one department and unlike jobs should be isolated from each other. All vagueness or overlapping jurisdictions should be removed by the Chief Executives, Departmentation depends upon the following factors:

(i) Work analysis.

(ii) Division of labour.

(iii) Specialisation.

Work analysis

Work analysis is an attempt to secure a number of close-up views of different operations and breaking down of each task into its component parts.

Work analysis is useful for simplifying the procedures and for ensuring improvement in various processes. It is also helpful for assessing each individual and department's achievement during a particular period. Moreover, the Chief Executive can on this basis plan in a better way.

In work analysis, all the possible jobs are listed and then the following data is secured:

1. How much time is spent by each individual in performing various jobs individually?
2. How much time is spent for each job by the whole staff?
3. How much does it cost in monetary terms?
4. How much amount is spent on various jobs individually?
5. How much amount is spent in providing a particular complete job?

Division of labour

After proper work analysis, each individual worker is assigned a particular job in accordance with his qualifications. The principle of division of labour is based on commonplace experience that every person cannot do every job. In other words, each person has generally more leanings towards one or the other aspect of a job. Some persons are prone to thinking, others are practical-minded and still others are found to be proficient in fine arts etc. To have an economical setup, it is a sound principle to divide the work into various work units and to assign the various identifiable jobs to individuals separately.

In a Technical Section of library, classification and cataloguing jobs are assigned to different persons. Still further division is done by assigning various component part jobs of cataloguing to various person e.g. by assigning the work of preparing the main entry cards to one person, of preparing the other added entries to the second and that of alphabetisation of cards to the third and that of filing cards to the fourth and so on and so forth.

Specialisation

Specialisation is another important principle by which a specific job is allowed to a specific person keeping in view his special qualifications and capacities. In a library, we may have competent cataloguers, classifiers and documentalists. So it will be for the benefit of the organisation to avail the services of specialists for doing specialised tasks.

Specialisation will ensure superior, economical, speedy and standards work since the same job done time after again, becomes a routine for the same person. He becomes perfect in doing it and does it speedily. Specialisation is very much desirable in bigger libraries for securing efficient and economical service.

Limited span of control

For efficient administration, there should be as few persons to be controlled directly by each head as is possible. In other words, there should be few sections under the charge of departmental heads to be directly controlled by the Chief Executive. If there are ten to fifteen departments, it is better to have two intermediary Deputy Chiefs so that the Chief Executive will have to deal with two Deputies only and in this way, he will be able to control the organisation easily. Similarly, in the Technical Section of a library where there are about twenty-five persons doing various jobs, it would be better to divide the department's work under two section heads e.g. Head of the Classification and Head of the Cataloguing Section. In this way, each section head will control few assistants and the department head will control the department through two section heads only.

Co-ordination

After establishing various departments, it becomes very essential that proper co-ordination between departments is ensured. In this way, the work is done smoothly without any friction. This can be achieved by the Chief Executive by holding regular meetings of the department heads. He should try to acquaint himself with the problems of various departments and the solution of the problems should be thrashed out in the meetings with the full concurrence of the department heads.

Leadership

The Chief Executive should have the qualities of a leader so that the subordinates derive inspiration from him. The Chief should be a hard worker and intelligent so that his subordinates follow him by example rather than by sermons since empty sermonising instead of having healthy effects lowers the prestige of the Chief. The Chief should be well-qualified, academically and professionally, so that the subordinates when confronted with various problems are able to seek solutions from the Chief. He should arouse amongst his subordinates interest and enthusiasm for the profession and loyalty to the organisation by his own example.

Facilitation

Proper arrangements should be made to secure adequate consultation and contact amongst the subordinates and high officials. In other words, the higher officials should be approachable to the subordinate officials also, so that their genuine difficulties are removed. It should be the objective of the organisation to save the organisation from strict regimentation. This can be achieved by holding general staff meetings on various occasions. The higher officials should utilise such occasions to acquaint themselves with the difficulties of the junior staff members.

Integration

Proper policy decisions must be taken by the Chief Executive so that the department heads are clear in their minds as to the extent of their authority to take certain decisions. For example, it is proposed by the Incharge Technical Section to introduce simplified cataloguing in place of descriptive cataloguing. This decision is going to have many repercussions in many departments. Whether the authority to take such decisions should be left to the department head of the Technical Section or the Chief Executives? Should the

Chief decide such important questions by himself or should these be decide in a meeting of senior staff members? Integration is the process by which scattered administrative agencies or activities are combined under central direction or control.

Parity of responsibility and authority

While devolving responsibility upon an official; care should be taken that he is bestowed with corresponding powers. In other words, the extent of authority should correspond to the amount of responsibility.

Library administration, if based on the above-mentioned principles, is bound to be successful. But the success of library administration depends upon the way these principles are practised and the manner in which the decisions are put into force. Expediency and tact are very important for this purpose.

In addition to these principles, the basic facts about a library must be taken into account while administering it. A library has got some difficulties and weaknesses. It is, on the whole, a dependent body. "It is likely to be a department of a larger organisation whose central executive usually tends to take advantage of his privileged position and develop a grasping tendency on the one hand and obstructive tactics on the other". Besides, a library is a 'spending body' and a 'growing organism'. Their implications must not be lost sight of.

Scientific management

Administration Vs. Management

Management is "the function...concerned in the execution of policy within the limits set up by Administration and the employment of the organisation for the particular objects before it". On the other hand, Administration is "the function... concerned in the determination of the corporate policy".

There are conflicting and confusing definitions of administration and management. To some 'Management' is a generic term while 'Administration' is considered only a part of the former. To others, 'Management' is a part of 'Administration". According to them, "that phase of a business enterprise which concerns itself with the overall determination of the major policies and objectives is Administration", while on the other hand, the function which concerns itself with the carrying out of the administrative policy laid down by Administration is 'Management'.

In spite of divergent opinions, 'management' is a very vital part in administration since it is "the art and science of organising and directing human effort applied to control the forces and utilise the materials of nature for the benefit of man'.

Nature of management

"Administration is becoming a science in our life-time.." Management, now -a-days, is a specialised job and it is not within the reach of the common man. It needs proper training and experience. It has a scientific character.

"Scientific management is the application of the principles and methodology of modern science to problems of administration". The motto of the Royal Society of London indicates the nature of modern science. It states, "Nothing on faith. If you want me to accept your view, prove that it's better than mine. I insist on evidence that is measurable". In other words, scientific management requires a complete mental revolution on the part of the workers and the management. Both must pay their whole-hearted attention towards increasing the size of the surplus. The old individual judgment or opinion must be replaced by exact scientific investigation and knowledge. Scientific management, in brief, involves certain combination of the following elements:-

1. Science instead of rule of thumb.
2. Co-operation instead of individualism.
3. Harmony instead of discord.
4. Maximum output instead of restricted output.
5. The development of each person to his greatest efficiency.

Necessity of Scientific Management

Frederick W. Taylor pointed out that the root cause of ills in management was ignorance on part of the management and the workmen. The former did not know as to what could be a fair day's work of a worker. They did not know as to how to convince the workers that they would get a fair reward for their efforts in production. The workers, on the other side, also were ignorant that they could secure a proper output if they were assured that they would get increased reward if the management earned more.

The necessity of following the principles of scientific management was explained by Taylor as follows:

1. That the whole country was suffering a great loss due to inefficiency found in their daily jobs.
2. That the remedy for curing it lay in providing systematic management.
3. That systematic management was a true science based on defined laws, principles and rules.

4. That these principles were applicable to all kinds of human activities.
5. That if and when these principles are applied correctly, the results must be very much encouraging.

He based his principles on Motion Study and Time Study.

Value of scientific management

Scientific management bestows certain important benefits upon those who practise it faithfully and sincerely. These are listed below:-

1. It helps in increasing efficiency and productivity.
2. It provides a scientific basis for fixing the wages of workers from time to time. The basis is the productivity in an enterprise.
3. It provides a valuable information and data about the desirability or otherwise of adopting rationalisation in an enterprise.

Limitations of scientific management

1. Scientific management is not an exact science because it deals with human beings. The human behaviour is variable. Human beings deal among themselves in the form of employers employees, customers and dealers etc. "Where human beings are concerned, management principles may be so much waste paper".
2. Every organisation has got its own traditions and objectives. Management principles, policies and techniques are applied to specific circumstances in each organisation. They invariably differ in each institution.
3. Science is advancing. So scientific management

must change from period to period. Those principles of scientific management which may be good today, may not be suitable tomorrow.

4. Work methods, work standards and output cannot be measured accurately and easily. Huge cost is involved in making these methods and standards foolproof.
5. The engineering side of the work is given undue emphasis while the human element, a basic factor in scientific management, is ignored to a great extent.
6. From workers' point of view, the scientific management means subjection of their work to their performance. They fear that it will lead to sending many of them out of job.

However, the benefits of scientific management outweigh its so-called demerits. Moreover, the demerits, if any, are remediable by judicious application of principles of scientific management and rationalisation. That is why the scientific management has been popular in almost all the advanced countries of the world. IT has been applied to almost all kinds of human activities.

Levels of management

Generally, there are three tiers of authority or management i.e. top, middle and lower. The top management includes the Chief Executive and other senior executives. In business enterprises these may be represented by the Managing Directors, General Managers or Presidents of the Boards of Management, and Deputy General Managers and Vice-Presidents etc. In Libraries, the Chief Librarians, Head Librarians or Directors of Libraries or Senior Professionals (Grade I) may represent the first type while the Deputy/Assistant Chief Librarians, Deputy/ Assistant Librarians or Deputy/Assistant Directors of Libraries or Senior Professional (Grade II) may be the second type. Similarly, the 'middle management' includes those persons through whom the Chief wields his authority and gets the jobs done. They include Heads of Departments and Superintendents. In libraries also they be called as Heads Incharge of particular Sections or Departments of a library. They may also be called as Junior Professionals. The lower management includes those person who directly supervise the work of the workers. In industrial organisations they may be called as General Foremen, Foremen and First-line Supervisors. In libraries, they may be called by various names e.g. Senior Library Assistants, Head Assistants, Office Superintendents and Library Assistants.

Functions

The functions of each of these three types of management may be as under:-

(a) *Top management*

(i) to take jurisdiction of an issue and to deliberate and decide;

(ii) to confirm the decisions taken by executives at different levels;

(iii) to counsel and guide them in initial stages of policy formulation; and

(iv) to review their acts through reports and inspection.

(b) *Middle management*

(i) to assist the chief executive;

(ii) to prepare themselves for undertaking broader responsibilities.

(iii) to understand others jobs and problems.

(iv) to serve as leaders for persons below them.

(v) to co-ordinate the activities in three directions i.e. upward, downward and sideward.

(c) Lower management

(i) to supervise the work of the rank and file.

(ii) to serve as administrative link between the workers and authorities.

(iii) to issue orders and directions to the workers to be implemented by them.

Principles of scientific management

Scientific management to be successful must be based on sound principles. Some of these principles may be as under:

1. *Job-analysis.* It is the determination of the jobs and their analysis into more or less independent sub-jobs. These jobs should not overlap each other in any way.

2. *Division of labour.* It is the determination of respective duties of personnel at various levels.

3. *Work methodology.* It means the improvement of methods of work. These should be based upon the tried systems such as time study, motion study and standardisation of tools, equipments etc.

4. *Maximum profits.* The organisation should be run on the most efficient lines so that there is maximum productivity for the employers and maximum prosperity for the employees.

5. *Incentive wage system.* The wage system must provide incentives to efficient workers so that they are encouraged to further improve their work.

6. *Complete Harmony.* There should be maximum harmony and co-operation between management and workers.

The basic principle of scientific management is the "distribution of responsibility or its decentralisation".

The top management confines itself to the formulation of policies and principles and deciding financial matters. The power of reviewing the execution of the policies etc. is left to the paid executives. The method of random sampling is used for reviewing purposes. The faults are corrected by scientific methods.

The executive officers, on the other hand, undertake full responsibility for carrying out faithfully the policies and principles laid down by the top management. The difficulties experienced by them in their day-to-day work are referred to committees appointed by the top management for necessary amendment or change in policies and principles.

Application of scientific management principles to libraries

The principles of scientific management can be profitably applied to the following library jobs which are amendable to proper analysis.

1. *Frequently performed* jobs such as duplicate checking, typing book orders, classifying, book numbering, reproducing cards, filing cards, book charging and discharging and book shelving.

2. *Repetitive jobs* involving recurrence of same steps each time a job is performed, such as book charging and discharging.

3. *Jobs requiring frequent movement of people or equipment* such as physical arrangement between acquisition and technical sections, public

catalogue, major bibliographical tools, reference, lending and circulation sections.

4. *Jobs with bottlenecks* such as delay caused in labelling or confusion in deciphering call numbers written in ink on the spines of books.
5. *Jobs involving large amounts of money* such as provision of reference service in a large library. Job-costing or cost-accounting is very useful in such a case.

Methodology and procedure of a scientific management study

A scientific management study should be entrusted to that person or body who has enough knowledge of the filed of investigation and the basic principles of scientific management.

Such a study involves the following steps:

1. *Defining the problem.* The scope of the problem should be clearly defined and understood.
2. *Gathering the data.* It is essential to know of what steps a job consists. In other words, the motion study must be made first. It should be followed by the time study i.e. the time required for performing each part of a job. Further, cost data for each item should be gathered.
3. *Analysing the present method.* The present method of analysis made use of should be properly understood in relation to each step of the process as well as the process as a whole. The following six steps can be useful in analysing a particular job:
   (i) Why is the job performed?
   (ii) What is the purpose of each step in relation to the purpose of the institution? What will it contribute to the overall process?

(iii) Where is the job done? Where else can it be performed?

(iv) When should the job be performed? Can it be performed at some other time with better results?

(v) Who should perform the job? Can it be performed by some other person with less qualification/training at less cost?

(vi How is the job performed? How could it be performed better?

4. *Developing an improved method.* An improved method can be developed in the following ways:

(i) By eliminating the whole or unnecessary process.

(ii) By combining various homogeneous process.

(iii) By changing the sequence or order of the processes.

(iv) By changing the operator.

(v) By simplifying the remaining processes.

5. Putting the improved method into operation. The improved method can be put into operation only when it is properly put to the supervisor. The supervisor should be co-operative. The following steps are involved in executing the improved method:-

(i) Presenting the new plan to the supervisor in writing.

(ii) Overcoming resistance from the supervisor and coworkers. The resistance is generally based on unfounded fear. The workers may feel that the new method may reveal that they were performing their jobs inefficiently; that they may be dismissed; or that their jobs may be considered superfluous and that as a result, they may be retrenched. For example, in India, at present, there is a strong opposition from workers to the introduction of computers in industry and business. The Life Insurance Corporation of India is experiencing such a resistance from its workers. Many people oppose the new methods for mere opposition. whatever the reason of such a fear may be, the innovator must understand the human nature and overcome the resistance with patience, perseverance, courage and wisdom.

6. *Training workers in the new processes.* In order to make the new process a success, the workers must be trained in making use of the new process.

7. *Initiating a trial operation and following it up.* Proper trials should be launched. These must be followed up vigorously. Nobody should be allowed to feel disappointed about the slow progress in the initial stages otherwise the workers would like to revert to their old methods.

Value of scientific management to libraries

Scientific management is not confined to industry and business alone. Rather it can be profitably made use of in public enterprises, may, even in public services also, which do not have a profit motive. The main advantages to libraries which partake the nature of a public service department may be as under:

1. *It helps in developing a factual data and argument.* A library has an onus to satisfy the tax-payer by providing him the maximum return for each rupee paid by him for library purposes. A

library is a growing organism and it needs additional funds year after year. The tax-payer wants to know why the additional amount is required. Not only an ordinary tax-payer but even experienced appropriating committees are impressed by quantitative and factual justification than eulogy of librarianship. Scientific management helps a librarian develop such a quantitative and factual argument in his favour for securing additional funds.

2. *It helps improve routine efficiency.* Majority of library tasks are of repetitive and mechanical nature and are amenable to quantitative analysis. These processes include ordering, cataloguing, card filing, binding, circulation and book shelving. Scientific management can enhance routine efficiency.

3. *It is a useful tool of library personnel management and financial administration.* Scientific management provides us work analysis of a job which is the key to modern job-classification. As a result of this analysis, the executive officer intelligently and precisely knows what he can and should expected from a worker. This provides him a yardstick to measure the work performed by a worker.

Similarly, scientific management helps an administrator run his business or organisation on sound financial lines. He knows the cost of each part of a job and thus he intelligently plans and avoids wastage and increases efficiency in service, thereby providing more satisfaction to his clients.

Rationalisation

Besides the rise of scientific management, the concept

of Rationalisation came to prominence in the twentieth century. This can also be useful to libraries.

Rationalisation was taken resort to in Germany after its industries had collapsed after World War I. It is "the employment of all means of technique and ordered plans which serve to elevate the whole industry and to increase production, lower its cost and improve its quality. The main aim of rationalisation is "to raise the general level of prosperity by cheaper, more plentiful and better quality goods". It means the application of rational methods i.e methods based on plausible reasoning and sound judgment. The elements of Rationalisation include the following:-

1. *It is a comprehensive process.* It does not deal with a problem piecemeal. Rather, on the other hand, it treats the problem as a whole. It implies careful planning in all phases of production, distribution and labour problems. Its aim is to improve these, thereby ensuring better quality goods and services at lower costs.

2. *Macro application.* It approaches the problems of an entire organisation rather than any one of its units singally. It implies the elimination of wastage either by winding up uneconomic units or amalgamating the latter with other units with an aim to ensure greater efficiency.

3. *Standardisation.* Rationalisation involves standardisation of products, services and means & processes of production and distribution.

4. *Mechanisation.* Rationalisation achieves its aims by the application of latest discoveries and inventions. It does this by the use of improved mechanical devices.

Advantages

The main advantages of rationalisation may be the following:-

1. It ensures better utilisation of resources/sources of production i.e. men, machines and materials.
2. It results in greater production of better quality goods and services.
3. The cost of production is lowered. Consequently, the prices are lowered. So the ultimate consumers are benefited.
4. The employees secure higher wages or remuneration.
5. As a result of the above, the overall effect is economic stability and industrial cooperation.

Its advantages

Rationalisation is not without some disadvantages. It may suffer from the following:-

1. Danger of over-production and consequent depression.
2. Monopolies may come up.
3. Weak and small units may face elimination.
4. Unemployment may spread.
5. The fruits of rationalisation can be reaped only if huge investment is made by installing latest and costly machines.

Conclusion

These disadvantages can be avoided only if rationalisation programmes are implemented with sincerity and confidence.

In India, though the Government of India and

other enterpreneurs are aware of the utility of rationalisation, yet so far it has not been applied much mainly due to the lack of increased finances and skilled labour.

The principles of rationalisation can be applied to libraries also with profit.

Library organisation versus library administration

Library organisation and library administration are related to each other so closely that it becomes sometimes difficult to make a clear-cut distinction between the two. Even the well-known librarians, authors and examiners confuse these two important subjects. A newcomer to the profession feels bewildered. This confusion is evident from examination question papers of various universities. Due to their close relation and perhaps due to non-existence of clear-cut distinction between the two, in Library Science courses of various universities, especially of the West, these two subjects are combined into one paper.

But if we go deep into the matter, we shall come to the conclusion that these two subjects are quite different even though the distinction is very subtle. One starts where the other ends. One is concerned with the laying down of theoretical principles whereas the other puts those principles into practice. The distinction between these two topics will become clearer if we define these two terms and find out their elements and functions respectively.

Organisation

Organisation is "the form of every human association for the attainment of a common purpose". "Organisation is the design of the structure, the grouping of positions, which will best carry out the library's planned objectives".

Organisation involves the designing of the structure of authority, defining and classing of posts, their relationship with each other and ensuring proper co-ordination for achieving the objectives of a library.

According to Gaus, White and Dimcock "organisation is the arrangement of personnel for facilitating the accomplishment of some agreed purpose through the allocation of functions and responsibilities. It is the relating of efforts and capacities of individuals and groups engaged upon a common task in such a way as to secure the desired objective with the least friction and the most satisfaction to those for whom the task is done and those engaged in the enterprise".

In other words, organisation means that:

1. There should be a common objective of an institution, and
2. All its members must subordinate their individual will to the common will. After the selection of proper staff, the directive function of the leader starts which is the province of administration.

Further, "Organisation implies the process of analysing into component parts and assembling the resultant units into a pattern for the attainment of the object in view".

"Organisation implies a structure of authority which requires a single directing executing authority and many workers. In setting up such an organisation one must

1. Define the objectives of the organisation very clearly;
2. Elect the leaders or directors of the enterprise who lay down the general policy of the enterprise in terms of the objectives;

3. Nominate the Managing Director or Chief Librarian whose task it is to see that the objectives are realised;
4. Determine the nature of the whole organisational framework, the number of specialised work units into which the task will have to be divided and the number of workers, as well as the various categories of workers required. Sub-division into sections, divisions or departments depends on the nature and extent of the task undertaken;
5. Establish and perfect the structure of authority between the managing director and the various work departments".

Administration

Administration involves the techniques by which the purpose of an organisation is fulfilled at minimum cost with minimum effort. Administration is, in fact, mainly concerned with the directive function through which an administrator unifies the efforts of all individuals engaged in an enterprise and guides their activities in the right direction. The administrator directs the energies of the personnel in the right channels so as to achieve the objectives for which the enterprise is brought into being, "Administration or direction is that function of management which actually executes or carries out the objectives for which the enterprise is organised. This function initiates the work to be performed, sees that personnel is fitted to the task, and trained to operate properly, and in general cases for everyday routine necessary to ensure that men, materials and equipment are functioning properly towards the desired end".

Administration concerns with following functions already explained in the foregoing pages:

1. Planning;
2. Organising;
3. Staffing;
4. Directing;
5. Co-ordinating;
6. Reporting; and
7. Budgeting.

The following devices and methods are used by an administrator for performing the above-mentioned functions:-

1. He provides for unit of management;
2. He divides the whole organisation into various departments;
3. He delegates authority to various units,
4. He finds out ways and means for proper co-ordination between various parts of the organisation;
5. He plans for keeping as limited span of control as is possible;
6. He works as leader of the organisation; and
7. He arranges periodical staff meetings, conducts inspections and issues administrative orders from time to time for smooth working of the organisation.

Distinction between library organisation and library administration

From the foregoing paragraphs, the functions of organisation and administration are crystal clear and their distinction from each other can be stated as under:

1. Organisation provides the structure of authority whereas administration actually uses the devices for achieving the objectives of an enterprise.
2. Organisation is "the machinery of administration, the channels through which the measures and policies of administration are put into effect". Administration, on the other hand, "is concerned with the directive function exercised by the leader of an enterprise".
3. An organisation comes first and administration follows it. In other words, there can be no efficient administration unless and until there is a sound organisation.
4. Administration starts the moment an organisation is established. A library is planned and established by utilising organising capacities of planners. The administration of the library starts when the day-to-day working of the library is to be undertaken. In other words, by administration is meant the practical techniques used for getting the work done in various departments of the library.
5. Organisation involves the theoretical aspects of ensuring an efficient and sound establishment, whereas the administration applies various principles for attaining the objectives of the organisation.

The difference between organisation and administration is very subtle. In fact, "both administration and organisation are merely the machinery for attaining an aim or objective".

Management by objectives (MBO)

The latest thinking about management is that best results can be achieved through management by objectives and as such it has now been accepted as the best management approach. The principles of this system were propounded in 1954 by Peter Drucker. It is based on two main principles:

(i) Results orientation; and

(ii) Particular view of human behaviour.

This system helps in realisation of an organisation's goals by its members as if those are their personal goals. The mechanism used to achieved the aims is that goal-setting process is made not only an open secret but all the members of the organisation are also made to realise the importance of the goals, thereby resolving the various inconsistencies and misunderstandings before these take firm roots. Any MBO system has four basic components:

1. Setting objectives.
2. Developing action plans.
3. Conducting periodic reviews, and
4. Appraising annual performance.

This system has been based on Maslow's theory of hierarchy of needs, and Herzberg's theory of identification of motivators and hygiene factors in the work environment. The former theory identifies two factors i.e.responsibility, achievement, and recognition while the latter takes into account better salary and other conditions of service. Besides McGregor's theory of management system and Likert's theory of participation fortify MBO theory. The first theory states that if employees are properly motivated to work, they are sure to be achievement-oriented. The second theory provides the mechanism of participative style of leadership and thus fosters commitment to objectives of an organisation..

Merits of system

The MBO system has the following seven benefits.

1. *Improvement in management performance*

It ensures managerial efficiency because manager's commitment to organisation's objectives increases as the members are made responsible for the achievement of their set objectives.

2. *Improvement in planning*

This is possible because each manager's individual goals are made consistent with those of each other and with those of the organisation because these are decided in the presence of their superiors.

3. *Improved co-ordination*

Improved planning and agreement on tapping of resources needed for the purpose result in better co-ordination of the organisation as a whole.

4. *Improved control*

Improved co-ordination results in improved control.

5. *Improved flexibility*

Each manager knows fully well his own objectives and those of the organisation and their priority for them, so improved flexibility is possible.

6. *Improved superior-subordinate relationships*

MBO provides increased opportunities for communication between the superiors and subordinates at various stages, such as at the time of objective-setting and performance appraisal.

7. *Improved personal development*

MBO provides better opportunities for personal development as it fosters personal responsibility.

Demerits of the system

Many writers have challenged MBO theory as enunciated by Maslow and Herzberg.

The main attack against the MBO theory is that it has been oversimplified and that the theory as enunciated by Herzberg is a theory of job satisfaction and not a complete theory of work motivation and improved job performance.

Second plank of attack is that MBO theory does not take into account other variables which affect job performance. For example, Victor Vroom gave three variables i.e. Valence, expectancy and force while according to Porter and Lawler these include efforts, performance, reward and satisfaction. Similarly, Smith and Cranny have proposed a three-pronged approach i.e. effort, satisfaction and reward.

The merits detailed above outweigh demerits because an organisation's inputs, outputs and processes are critically examined through self-analysis. This is the main reason why MBO theory is respected inspite of severe criticism against it.

MBO's relevance to libraries

Libraries can benefit from MBO though in a limited way. MBO is relevant to various technical and procedural operations in Libraries such as acquisition processes and technical services. MBO is beneficial to middle management of library. In other words, it is relevant to Sectional and Departmental Heads. It is useful for libraries because a library can be managed by sharing responsibility among those who are responsible for managing a library. However, those benefits which are likely to accrue from MBO approach should be carefully weighed keeping in view the staff and monetary costs.

5

Preparing for Library Leadership

Many libraries today are engaging in strategic planning, scenario building, and other future-oriented exercises. They are trying to understand the future, so that they can prepare themselves with the right combination of skills and resources to meet its challenges. Leadership is one such resource, and the need to focus on its role within the library profession is critical.

Leadership

The question continues on where and how we find leaders. There is a body of literature on the study of leadership which explore whether leaders are born or made, whether leadership is a collection of traits that a person has or whether leadership is a collection of traits that a person has or whether leaders emerge from a unique situation or circumstance.

The methodology used by two sets of researchers includes interviews with and observation of acknowledged leaders, as well as discussions with their peers, associates, subordinates and bosses. They examined what characteristics these individuals displayed that lead others to reorganise them as leaders and how these characteristics manifested themselves.

Although described in different words, both studies identify five strategies employed by these individuals: vision, communication, trust, risk, and empowerment.

The ability to see or to imagine a future that goes beyond what others believe possible was primary characteristic of the individuals identified by these two groups of researchers. The direction their enterprise should take and the view of what the best possible future should look like was crystal clear. The compelling nature of their vision provided a hook on which other could hang their commitment, their loyalty, and their own sense of purpose.

The capacity to envision a unique image of an ideal future is crucial to leadership but meaningless without the ability to communicate that vision. So much of what is truly innovative and has the potential to reshape our views is lost through an inability to be articulate, to fire the imagination of others. The leaders in this study were those who were able to get the people around them to commit to and support their vision.

A high level of trust is needed to take individuals and an enterprise through an ambiguous period of transition into an uncertain future. One way that leaders are able to inspire others to do new thing or act in unaccustomed ways for a greater good is by modeling a particular set of behaviours themselves. Individuals reported that part of their willingness to follow their leader in new directions was derived from his or her demonstrated personal commitment to a goal through consistent, personal efforts.

Leaders are also identified by others as those who challenge the status quo, experiment, and take risks. This does not seem to come as much from a desire for excitement as from a desire to learn. Learning is seen as a requirement for growth and change. The leaders in these two studies showed a bias towards action and viewed the mistakes they made and those made by others as part of the learning process.

Partly a strategy in itself and partly the logical result of the other four strategies, individuals around these described leaders felt strengthened by his or her actions and through his or her presence. When leaders create a vision that is a true reflection of the values, needs, and desires of those they intend to lead, their followers feel supported on a very deep level. They are more able to commit to and work toward the goals that have been articulated. They feel challenged and derive a greater sense of meaning from their work.

In combination, these five strategies provide us with a model for understanding leadership. One of its strengths is that it makes sense. Some of us watch leadership from afar as it operates in society at large. Others have been lucky enough to work with a true leader and have been able to observe these actions close at hand. For most of us, this conceptual framework matches with our personal experience.

The question still remains as to whether individuals armed with these strategies can provide libraries with the kind of leadership that will be needed to take them into the twenty-first century. To answer this, a better understanding of our anticipated future is required.

The future

We look around and we can all see changes and trends that will have an impact on the way we operate both personally and professionally in the future. Gareth Morgan and Joseph Johnston Jr. have identified a number of these trends from which we have chosen those that we believe have the greatest relevance for libraries. Other eras have experienced enormous changes brought on by social, economic and technological developments. The difference today is that, along with the complex and large-scale character of the changes facing us, the rapid rate and ongoing nature of these change processes leave us with a sense of constantly being in a state of flux or transition.

Libraries will have to be prepared to add and eliminate services and technologies as need and demand shift. Library organisations were designed to produce a consistent, quality product-retrievable materials. Our structures will have to be revamped to permit us to be more responsive to these shifts.

Libraries have always been in the business of collecting organising and facilitating access to knowledge. The information explosion has already had an enormous impact on the ability of libraries to maintain these traditional functions. We must prepare ourselves as society refocuses its attention and energy into an area that has traditionally been our private domain. We have always seen information as an inexhaustible resource. More and more, we are hearing it described and used as a commodity.

We except and our clients except that libraries will continue to offer the same, high quality services that have been offered in the past. The quandary arises when opportunities for new or improved service present themselves. With little or no more money being added to base budgets, it is difficult to see how new programs can be created and the same standards of quality maintained.

A larger number of groups of individuals are being recognised as having a stake in the success or failure of an enterprise's endeavors. They can include the staff, the clients, and the suppliers. Organisations are beginning to learn to exploit their commitment by giving them a larger role in functioning of the organisation.

In libraries, we find staff want to be more involved in decisions that will affect the quality of their work life. Libraries are looking to publishers to recognise the partnership in which we're engaged in order to be more influential in the choice of paper used in book publishing of the price of serials.

The changing nature of work and the decentralisation of power has lead to organisations that are less hierarchical. The increased interdependence of the various units requires a greater emphasis on collaboration and a need for more and better communication structures.

The use of groups in the management processes of libraries has grown phenomenally over the past fifteen years. Traditionally, the role of the middle manager was to pass information up and down through the organisation. With increased access to information at all levels through local computer systems, organisational structures are likely to continue to flatten.

The problems that face libraries now and that will confront them in the future will continue to grow more complex. They will require a variety of perspectives to understand and solve them, involving more people in the process. As the choices grow more difficult to make, a greater willingness to take risks will be necessary to avoid paralysis and to develop the kinds of innovative solutions that will be needed. Most library reward systems do not currently support these needs. By focusing only on successful completion of tasks, they discourage attempts to try new approaches which traditionally have greater potential for failure.

By developing our ability to understand and anticipate the future through the analysis of current trends, we also enhance our ability to influence the future. Organisations can no longer afford to merely manage what happens to them. They have a responsibility to increase their effectiveness by trying to shape and influence the elements within their environment.

From these projections, we can begin to develop a picture of the kinds of knowledge or skills our leaders will need in order to meet these challenges. First and foremost is the ability to deal with ambiguity, to function effectively in situations where the rules and boundaries are not clear. Because there will be so few anchors, the ability to make choices and focus energy, (one's own and that of others), will also be important.

Most efforts will be collaborative, rather than individual. An understanding of group dynamics and strong interpersonal skills will be essential to effective functioning. These group activities and the multiple constituencies we anticipate will make the ability to communicate clearly critical to personal and organisational success.

The leaders the library profession will need in the future must be able to employ the same strategies identified by the leadership studies already mentioned. Because of the ambiguous, uncertain nature of the future that we face, we will need leaders who are willing to take some risks and try new things. One of those risks will be making a commitment to a particular course of action and focusing the energy on an entire enterprise on the accomplishment of that goal.

In order to do that, out leaders will have to share their vision; they will need to communicate effectively their sense of purpose to others. They must possess both a good knowledge of individuals and groups and an understanding of what motivates them to make strengths of others and how to build on those strengths. They need to make people feel uplifted, not diminished, by their commitment to an enterprise, a course of action, and a vision of the future.

Learning to be leaders

There are three issues to be considered in leadership training: what needs to be learned, where it should be learned, and how it should be learned. It the second part of this chapter, we will focus on specific competencies of leadership and how they might be nurtured within library organisation.

If we examine current research on how individuals become effective managers, we can find clues that will help up to develop models for effective leadership training libraries. By examining life histories, researchers at CCL were able to identify four arenas that play a major role in the development of successful, high-level executives. They were challenging assignments, other people, hardships and significant events.

Challenging assignments included starting something from scratch, cleaning up a messy situation, taking on a project or being a part of a task fore team, increasing responsibility, and switching from a line to a staff position. There were two ways in which other people had an impact on the development of these individuals: both negative and positive role models were identified; and memorable events of short duration, both positive and negative, demonstrating the impact of interpersonal interactions were described.

The kinds of hardships identified by the CCL study were errors in judgment or mistakes that led to failure, problem staff, having to starting over in a new job or career, and personal traumas. They also included career crises, such as demotions, being passed over for promotion, and lousy jobs- specifically, a job that was different from what was anticipated or desired. Other significant events included courses and formal training programs, early work experiences, (especially first supervisory experiences), and an array of personal experiences that took place outside of the work environment.

The CCL study sought to discover how these executives learned to be effective or discovered an ability to be effective through these experiences. Participants in the study identified the lessons they believed they earned from these events. The lessons were clustered then correlated with the appropriate event to see which experience seemed to have the greatest impact on the learning of a particular lesson.

We have already identified the strategies connected with leadership behaviour. Let us now explore the relationship between what these executives felt they learned from their experience and what we want out leaders to know or know how to do.

Development leadership competencies

Part of the utility of CCL's study is that it helps us to analyse how the competencies that lie behind the leadership strategies could be consciously developed. If we can identify at least some of the components that support and individual's ability to behave in a desired way, then we can develop activities that will enhance that ability.

The ability of focus purpose into a unique, meaningful vision that can be acted upon is the characteristic most often identified with leaders. In many ways this is very similar to what the CCL study called setting and implementing agendas. Four of the lessons related to this quality would be useful in developing visionary potential: knowledge of technical/professional content, understanding how the business works, strategies thinking, and innovative problem-solving methods.

Moving from a line to a staff position was the experience that had the biggest impact on learning in these four areas. It helped the individual to develop a greater appreciation for other areas within their organisation. Staff were also able to develop skills, such as planning, financial analysis, and human resources development that encourage and support a border perspective. Outside coursework was also useful in supporting the development of technical or professional knowledge.

If we wish to construct developmental activities such as these in libraries, there are some key elements to build in and some to avoid. An effective staff assignment should be relatively short, about a year, and involve some form of organisational analysis to encourage abstract thinking.

Strategic planning is ideal, but projects that focus on financial analysis or program development could serve the same purpose. During this process, the individual should report to someone higher up on the organisation. This special reporting relationship makes the experience more meaningful by providing access to feedback that is broader in nature and gives the individual a greater sense of contribution. Routine jobs in personnel and administration do not provide the same kind of the developmental growth.

Two other experiences that support growth in this

arena are opportunities to start something from scratch and to fix something that's gone awry. As technology changes what is done in libraries and how it is done, we have more opportunities to provide start-up projects for those identified as having leadership potential. Developing new services for the public and new internal processes and procedures fit into this category. The critical elements are that the individual take full responsibility for the success or failure of the operation and that they work through the constraints and the pressures on their own.

There are always areas in our libraries that are not working as productivity of efficiently as possible, and sometimes there are areas that need or efficiently as possible, and sometimes there are areas that need a complete overhaul. Rather than allowing these units to languish, the situation can provide an excellent opportunity to develop diagnostic skills and abilities. Individuals engaged in these kind of undertakings learn the importance of careful analysis before action.

It seems that most of our approaches to problem-solving are developed during our earliest work experiences. Libraries that wish to encourage innovative thinking can assist staff by offering training in creative problem-solving techniques. These techniques can be institutionalised through effective meeting planning and their use encouraged throughout the organisation.

Kouzes and Posner report that, based on their study of leadership, "inspiration" is the most difficult competency to learn. If we approach it from a pragmatic point of view, this issue relates most closely to communication and influencing skills. In the CCL study, the sections which dealt with handling relationships contain some data on influencing, but communication is not directly addressed. Getting others to implement your solutions was most often learned from the earliest supervisory experience. The lesson was that in working with people, the people themselves are the key to success.

There are many projects in libraries that require "but-in" by, multiple constituencies, such as reorganisations, bringing up an online catalog, introduction of fees for services, and changes in performance evaluation systems. These kinds of assignments provide opportunities for potential leaders to make the connection between their ability to communicate the importance and benefits of an endeavor and its successful outcome.

The most critical step in the process of enlisting the support of others is understanding the group or groups with which one is working. In order to be convincing, one must know what ideas and ideals are held in common. In order to tap into these commonalities, we must know their values, what they believe in. The need for an analytical approach must be continually understood.

We have all seen situations where a project was undermined because the appropriate level of the energy and commitment had not been elicited from those who had to make the operational effort. Potential leaders must learn how hat advance preparations need to be made to ensure a successful change operation. If we want staff to develop in this area, we must give them feedback on their communication strategies, rather than evaluating them simply on the content.

We should provide critical feedback in terms of the mechanics of the communication process. The message should be repeated a number of times, in different ways, so that as many people as possible can be reached in as many different ways as possible. Examples of what the new approach has to offer should be credible and vivid, positive and hopeful, and passionate. People want to succeed and forms of formal and informal communication should make them feel included in the vision. Formal and informal courses can also aid in the development of effective oral and written communication skills.

The trust of other and self-confidence go hand in hand. It is difficult for other to trust us and have confidence in us if we do not have confidence in ourselves. How did the participants in the CCL study think that they developed confidence?

Surprisingly, the mechanism most often mentioned was coursework, with participation in projects and task force a close second. Through courses, individuals are exposed to information and experiences not available in the workplace, The knowledge should be both conceptual and technical in nature. Classes also provide opportunities for self-assessment: sorting out personal strengths and weaknesses, as well as objective comparison with others. Supporting coursework through release time and direct financial aid is a way for organisations to show their support for individual development.

Projects and task force assignments provide the same kind of proving ground that formal coursework offers and can be designed to deliver a high level of development impact. A tight time frame forces staff to get up speed quickly. The small group size ties the success and failure more closely to the individuals working on the project, If the project requires dealing with a variety of groups, the team members learn not only to coordinate their work with each other, but to negotiate relationships with those outside the group, as well.

Bennis and Nanus also identify visible, tangible personal commitment to an idea or project as one of he elements that leads people to trust a leader. In CCL's study, the lesson of singleness of purpose and standing up for one's beliefs were most often derived from adverse conditions or situations.

Risk is defined as the exposure to a chance of loss. Our ability to take risks comes in part from our desire to do something different or in a different way, recognising and seizing opportunities, and having the confidence to stand along and act. Learning to final alternatives in solving and framing problems seems to come mostly from early work experiences.

Taking full responsibility was also one of the lessons learned through setting and implementing agendas. Participants felt they learned it from all their experiences but most often it was learned in the process of cleaning up a mess and starting something from scratch. Decision making was the skill they felt they'd acquired, and a bias for action was the attitude that went with it.

Being prepared to take advantage of the unexpected was learned from difficult situations that forced the individual to exchange the known for the unknown. Situations that could foster this lesson are those that encourage an individual to move from an area with which he or she is comfortable and familiar, into an area where they do not have the same level of expertise. We do not take nearly as much advantage of job exchange programs as we could in this regard. A successful outcome will support independent risk taking in the future.

No one wants to fail or to see others fail. One of the problem with developing risk taking potential is that, in trying to protect ourselves and others from failure, we often become overly cautious and conservative in our approach. Even with all our precautions, each of us at some point in the past has made a mistake, missed an opportunity, or been the victim of unfortunate circumstances.

How the organisation deals with these kinds of situations is the key to what learning is acquired from them. The lesson can be "don't ever try that or anything like that again until you're sure," or it can be "let's find out why that didn't work, so that we can try something else that might."

Rosabeth Kanter has described empowerment as a process that makes power widely accessible within an organisation. Her studies have shown that organisations which support. A leader can only empower other to the degree to which he or she is willing to share these commodities.

Some of those who reported about their experiences in the CCL study learned lessons that apply to the development of this competency. These include politics as a part of organisational life, the use and abuse of power, discovering that a single person cannot do it all alone, understanding the perspective of others, and finding out how to develop others. Almost all of these lessons were reported to have come from hardship experiences, from failures, demotions, and personal trauma. To a lesser degree, increased responsibility also contributed to these leanings.

There are few who would argue that we should create situations for people to fail, so that they could derive the appropriate lessons from them. The critical factor in dealing with these experiences is learning how to learn from them. Postmortems are routinely done when someone dies, not to find fault, but to understand why it happened. There are many lessons to be learned when something does not go as expected or hoped.

We do not wish to stifle the individual creativity and initiative that leads to vision and risk taking in the process of developing empowerment skills. We do, however, want to find ways to help our potential leaders recognise that other have the same desire to contribute as they do. As can be seen from CCL's study, one of the most poignant ways that individuals learn this lesson is by trying to do things along and failing. The true failure is in not recognising the potential of others.

6

Administrative Data Processing

Before proceeding, however, let us fit each of those subsystems into the framework of a total library system schematic, so that the interrelationships among subsystems can be kept in mind as we consider each in turn. The library system schematic consists of seven major functional subsystems (administrative, ordering, cataloging, circulation, serials, interlibrary loan, and information services) considered at four levels of processing (administrative, financial, mechanical, and intellectual).

Functional division. The division into functional subsystems is fairly obvious and consistent with the usual pattern of looking at library operations, except perhaps for the information services subsystem. This one arises from the new opportunities for service which data processing technology provides, especially through the increasing availability of nationally produced magnetic tape data files. The others are simply more or less traditional parts of library technical services and library management.

Levels of processing. The division into levels of processing provides a relatively simple way of distinguishing between those kinds of processing which are more or less comparable to processes in business (administrative and financial), those which are specialised to library operation but still purely clerical or mechanical, and those with a high degree of intellectual content.

Format for system description

Background: This will present a description of the general nature of the sub-system, with emphasis on its role in the library and on the functional requirements it must satisfy. Specific criteria, both quantitative and qualitative, will be presented for evaluation of alternative methods of meeting those requirements.

Forms and files. Then the various forms and files involved in the subsystem will be described, and the general character of file management functions associated with their maintenance and use will be discussed.

Illustrative systems. For each subsystem, the experience will be presented of various libraries which have had operational use of computers.

Parameters for estimation. For each subsystem, parameters relevant to estimation of processing times and costs will be presented. Where it is possible to do so, representative values will be provided. In addition, as discussed later, an illustrative example will be used and the estimates implied by it will be listed as well.

Alternative configurations of equipment

To provide some picture of the nature of the alternatives for each subsystem, we will consider three levels and kinds of installation-a small library-based batch processing computer system; a larger batch processing system; and a very large on-line system. Each of the latter two is representative of what might be available from a parent organisation or a commercial service bureau.

Small-scale library-based facility. Figure 1 lists a typical small -scale facility, suitable for consideration by a library large enough to justify its own equipment. The internal memory limits the complexity of process which can be handled,, and computers of this general size can perform only about 10,000 operations per second (e.g., 100 microsecond add time). The operation must therefore be oriented around batch processing, with extensive card handling.

The external file equipment which can be used with such computers tends to be limited both in capacity and in data transfer rates. The magnetic tape they use, for example, will store about 10 million characters, and the tape handlers will transfer data at only 15,000 to 20,000 characters per second, magnetic discs will store about 5 million characters with random access time of about 0.1 second. However, the other peripheral equipment-printers, card devices, etc.-are comparable to those which larger computers will use.

Figure 1: Small scale batch processing computer. In a small-scale facility, terminal equipment and communications line charges will arise only from the circulation control subsystem and will function off-line

Equipment components	*Monthly costs*
Computer (with 16,000 characters of internal memory)	$1,800
Card, input, output, and handling	500
Terminal equipment	1,000
Printer (500 lines per minute)	500
Magnetic tape handlers	2,000
Magnetic disk unit	1,000
Communication lines key punch units	200
	$7,000

Personnel	*Monthly salaries*
Operating personnel	$3,900
Supervisory	1,200
	$5,100
Overhead (at 50 percent of total salaries)	2,550
	$7, 650

Large-scale batch processing facility. Figure 2 lists a typical large-scale facility, suitable for use in a fairly large organisation. Only the very largest libraries could justify a dedicated facility of this size, but many libraries will have such facilities available to them from their parent organisations or commercial service bureaus. The internal memory is large enough to handle even very complex tasks. The operating speed (typically about 20 microsecond add time) is fast enough for a limited degree of "on-line processing", but for processing efficiency such systems are primarily used for large-scale batch operations. External files can be maximum performance units with large capacities and high data transfer rates-up to 150,000 or even 350,000 characters per second.

Figure 2: Large-scale batch processing computer. Terminal equipment is limited to circulation transactors and a few on-line typewriters

Equipment components	*Monthly costs*
Computer (with 128,000 characters of internal memory)	$ 5,000
Card input, output, handling	1,500
Terminal equipment	2,000
Printer	800
Magnetic tape handlers	4,000
Magnetic disk units	4,000
Communication controls	1,500
Keypunch units	1,000
	$19,800

Personnel	*Monthly salaries*
Operating personnel	$12,000
Supervisory	4,000
	$16,000
Overhead (at 50 percent of total salaries)	8,000
	$24,000

Large-scale on-line processing system. Figure 3 lists a very large-scale, very high-speed system, representing the kind of equipment on which most of the speculation about the future role of computing is based. It would be found in very large companies, in large universities, in a computer "utility". Particularly as the latter becomes a reality, libraries of all sizes may find themselves using such facilities. The size of memory is large enough to handle multiprocessing of several tasks at the same time, many of them on-line and even interactive, and many of them batch. The speed of operation (with add times of 1 or 2 microseconds) is fast enough to meet all the needs of on-line processing of several simultaneous users. The peripheral equipment, magnetic tapes, and magnetic disks will have the highest possible performance. A complete installation will even include one or more subsidiary computers operating under the control of the master computer.

Figure 3: Large-scale on-line computer. Communication line charges depend upon the volume of traffic and the geographic distances

Equipment components	*Monthly costs*
Computer (with 1,000,000 characters of internal memory)	$50,000
Peripheral input-output (card equipment, printers, etc.)	10,000
Terminal equipment	10,000
Magnetic tape handlers	10,000
Magnetic disk units	20,000

Communication line	
Communication controls	10,000
Subsidiary, slave computers	30,000
	$140,000

Personnel	*Monthly salaries*
Operating personnel	$37,000
Systems programming personnel	20,000
Supervisory personnel	13,000
Overhead (at 50 percent of total salaries)	70,000
	35,000
	$105,000

These three facilities differ significantly in their efficiency (cost-effectiveness) as well as their inherent capacity for processing and file storage. Since, in this chapter and the succeeding ones, we will make rough comparisons of their relative performance on library subsystems, it is useful to summarise some representative data about these differences in capacity. These will necessarily be much simplified and therefore should be regarded only as illustrative. However, care has been taken to assure that they are at least reasonably close to reality.

One primary issue in evaluating processing capacity is the time for sorting.

Another primary issue is the time for processing a simple "record up-date". In general, a transaction will affect several totals recorded in the stored records involved. The time to carry out the simple computations is therefore dependent upon the basic add time of the computer and the number of totals affected. A typical "record-update operation" is diagrammed in fig. Included are estimates of the time for executing such an operation.

Normally, the easiest of all computer system

running times to estimate are those timings occurring as a result of input or output. The estimate is calculated as an elementary division problem, in which the volume of input or output (in cards, or lines, or characters) is simply divided by the rated speed of the input or output device.

Another issue affecting processing capacity is the degree of independence among components-to what extent each component is "tied-up" of committed during the execution times of other components. For example, during the time required for card input, the card reader is of course completely committed, but the computer may be committed for only a percentage of the same time. The size of that percentage depends in part upon the availability of independent buffers, controls, and communication lines, and in part upon the number of independent tasks which can be processed at the same time. In general, of course, the larger the computer, the greater the degree of independence in operation. Basically, the small-scale batch computer allows a bare minimum of independent operation, especially in the context of library tasks, which involve primarily input-output and file handling operations with only limited processing. The large-scale batch computer may have capacity for as many as 10 simultaneous tasks-with the library only one of the users-and can provide a high degree of independent operation of peripheral equipment; on the average, due to variation in work load, it might be expected that five tasks will be processed simultaneously. The large-scale on-line computer has capacity for perhaps 50 simultaneous tasks, although again on the average, only 25 might be processed at a time.

Roughly, the three facilities will compare with one another in approximately the ratio shown as follows:

Comparison of computer systems

	Cost	*Computing capacity*	*File capacity*	*Input-output capacity*
Small-scale batch	1	1	1	1
Large-scale batch	3	10	10	5
Large-scale on-line	20	400	100	25

Above figure presents a summary of typical characteristics for the three levels of equipment, including estimates of the degrees of independence and resulting basis for charging for computer time. We will use these in subsequent estimates for the processing times and costs of various levels of computer-facilities on each library subsystem.

For purposes of testing the approach to estimation and for comparison with the computer based methods, it is useful to evaluate a manual system and a punched card system.

Assignment of responsibilities

The issue of excess capacity (or even, in some cases, deficiencies in capacity) implicitly raises a most important consideration, relevant to each of the subsystems being considered. Who does what? Libraries rarely exist independent of other institutions. In fact, usually they are a part of some larger organisation, with its own data processing requirements and frequently even its own installation of data processing equipment. A most significant decision then is which functions, if any, are to be handled on the library's own, dedicated equipment, which are to be handled on those of the parent organisation, and which may be contracted to commercial service bureaus.

This issue is most evident with respect to the subsystem to be considered in this chapter-the administrative subsystem. Frequently, if not usually, there will not even be a decision problem: The parent organisation traditionally assumes responsibility for all administrative, financial, and managerial accounting. In fact, since this is so frequently the case, it might be considered that the administrative subsystem is irrelevant to library data processing. However, the issue of system evaluation is still relevant, wherever the processing will be done. Furthermore, the library has its own needs for administrative data and must be clearly aware of the nature of the data processing requirements they present, even if they may satisfied elsewhere. For the other subsystems, on the other hand, the decision problem is highly relevant.

Administrative data processing subsystem

It is useful to start out discussions of library subsystems with administrative data processing because, of all of them, it is most nearly comparable to those one finds in a typical small business. There is therefore a considerable amount of existing expertise, procedures, experience, and basis for evaluation on which to draw. On the other hand, there is remarkable lack of descriptive information concerning library administrative data processing recorded in the library literature. It is almost as though it were regarded as beneath the librarian's position to be concerned with such mundane issues as personnel records, payroll, purchasing, and accounting. Yet, the facts are that whether or not the librarian himself is responsible for the actual data processing work in these areas, the ways in which they are done have direct and immediate impact on the library and its professional responsibilities.

General nature of administrative data processing

The files and functions in administrative data processing can be conveniently grouped into three categories: (a) those concerned with financial issues, (b) those concerned with personnel, and (c) those concerned with management.

Financial issues. The librarian is responsible for management of an accounting for a number of kinds of funds-book funds, expenses, capital investment, etc. He must prepare a budget to cover the library's requirements for funds, control the way in which that budget is spent, pay for what is received, and be accountable for the results. Accounts must be kept which record all sources of income and disbursements of funds; books and supplies must be purchased, and the vendors must be paid; reports must be prepared to describe and to justify how money was used; and the data from past experience must be used to determine what future requirements will be. All of this requires the maintenance and use of files of data.

Personnel issues. The library is staffed with professional librarians, technical personnel, clerks, and hourly employees. They must be hired, assigned to work, and paid: their costs must be allocated to one or another financial account. Reports must be made to the government and to library management. All of this also requires the maintenance and use of files of data.

Management issues. The management of a library requires data which can only be obtained from the processing of large quantities of data-inventory control, cost accounting, assignment of work loads and planning for production, maintenance of statistics for measurement of performance. Again, as we will discuss, this requires the maintenance and use of files of data.

Qualitative character of the library

In reviewing these aspects of administrative data

processing, there are some special characteristics about the library which must be kept in mind.

Nonprofit. Most libraries (and especially public, school, and academic research libraries) are nonprofit organisations. As a result, some of the practices appropriate to profit-making corporations are simply not applicable. This has been most evident in the historic differences in handling direct and indirect costs, with nonprofit corporations tending to put a far higher percentage of expenditures into direct costs. It also shows up in the infrequent use of depreciation in library accounting, presumably because, in contrast to a business, there is no reason for interest in the tax advantages which depreciation offers.

Service. Libraries are service institutions and, in fact, provide a most intangible kind of service-information. There are therefore significant differences from the accounting practices in manufacturing organisations. To an `extent, there are now appearing on the scene commercial organisations with comparable accounting needs-the computer service bureaus, the "information industry", etc.

Nonindependence. Few libraries exist as independent entities. Each is a part of a university, a governmental agency, a school, a company. The accounting practices they must follows are almost certain to be those of the parent institution. In fact, as we have pointed out, usually they will be carried out by the parent institution itself.

Quantitative character of the library

Some perspective on the sizes of libraries can be provided by the comparison, of libraries in general with manufacturing companies. As it shows, libraries are really quite small in size, a large library having a staff of 500 to 1000 (and a budget of only $5 million to $10 million). As a result, if only the standard accounting functions were being considered, at most a small level of computing capacity would be required. This will become very clear as we consider the work load represented by, for example, the library's payroll.

On the other hand, the services of the library involve a high work load of data processing, especially in terms of the sizes of files. For example, the catalog of a library can be as large as 10 to 10 characters-a size which stretches the capacity of present technology. Even operations such as serial records maintenance, which is somewhat analogous to inventory control, are much larger processing tasks than their counter parts in manufacturing companies of comparable size. As a result, data processing is certain to be considerably more expensive for a library than it will be for an industrial concern. In a sense, it becomes comparable to mechanising the manufacturing plant and not just the paperwork.

Financial data processing

Financial data processing involves the normal accounting or bookkeeping functions, the control of purchasing, and the payment of bills. The objective is to maintain a record of each and every expenditure against a library budgetary account. Each fund must be encumbered at the time even a tentative commitment is made, and then the records must be reconciled with the actual amounts paid against invoices or vouchers. The library accounting modules therefore must maintain a record of expenditures against each library account. Major library accounts should be subdivided into allocations small enough for control by organisational units assigned responsibility for specific categories of expenditures. To make this effective, regular, periodic reports must be prepared for each of these organisational units, to assist them in their efforts to control expenditures and the accounting structure must be coordinated with the budgeting format.

Means should be provided for projecting probable patterns of expenditure through the end of the fiscal year, based on historical experience. To do so, the accounting module should provide a variety of special statistical summaries as required during the year.

Forms and files

Figure 4 lists some of the forms and files required in a library accounting subsystem. One is central-the Balance Sheet Accounts File. It is the ultimate means by which the library controls the distribution of funds. The results of all financial transactions must be recorded in this file, and the data stored in it becomes the basis for all estimations of budget. The other forms and files control the commitment and payment of funds to agencies outside the library.

Figure 4: Forms and files in accounting modules

F_1	Balance Sheet Accounts File
F_2	Purchase Order File
	Purchase Order Form
	Voucher Form
F_3	Accounts Payable File

Bookkeeping. The balance sheet accounts file stores financial data in considerable detail, for the library as a whole as well as for separate library subdivisions and departments, by budgetary classes. Figure 5 lists typical budgetary classes (bookkeeping accounts). A chart of accounts might include as many as 40 or 50 separate records for each of 20 or 30 library subdivisions and departments, (a file totaling about 164,000 characters). If separate book fund accounts are included here in addition to being part of the book ordering subsystem, they could add another 100 or 200 records. These records are used to provide accounting of expenditures in comparison with the budget, by time period. For purposes of budgetary control and estimation of future budgets, a variety of reports are produced, showing variances from the budget in comparison with previous time periods and planned expenditure rates.

One crucial concept in modern systems for providing such information to management is the use of "exception reporting". The aim is to place as much of the burden of pinpointing problem areas on the computer. Thus, if expenditure rates in a given budgetary account are within reasonable limits of the planned rates, there is little reason to do more than report that fact. But where they differ significantly from planned rates., management should be alerted. This is best done by a report which includes only the exceptions, the departures from expectation, the problem areas.

Figure 5: Representative bookkeeping accounts

Salary related accounts	*Office expenses accounts*
Salaries	Postage
Payroll taxes	Telephone and communication
Pension fund	Office services
Insurance	Office equipment, purchase
Social security	Office equipment, rental
Supplies accounts	*Facility accounts*
Office supplies	Rent
Book preparation supplies	Utilities
Automative supplies	Construction materials
Building maintenance supplies	Motor vehicles
Printing and reproduction accounts	*Book accounts*
Office copying equipment	*Financial accounts*
Printed forms	Cash

Reports	Accounts payable Accounts receivable Depreciation

Figure 6: Bookkeeping reports

1. Trend reports, comparing activity over a period of time.
2. Analytical reports, analysing changes.
3. Comparison reports among departments.
4. Percentage expenditure analysis.

The sources of data include budgets for each department, records of appropriations of funds, purchase orders and other commitments, vouchers or invoices and other records of actual payments, and records of prior history. The çomputer processing itself is relatively uncomplicated, involving simply double-entry posting of changes to accounts with additions to and subtraction from existing amounts.

Purchasing. The function of the "purchasing module" is to control the extent of commitments against library funds for other than acquisitions (the Ordering subsystem covering the commitments against book funds). It includes checking requisitions and orders, securing quotations where necessary, issuing purchase orders, scheduling deliveries, checking receipts and verifying invoices and corresponding with vendors. Each record represents an outstanding purchase order, against which receipts are to be matched. As ordered items are received, they must be checked against the purchase order for both quantity and quality; the prices, terms, and discounts on the invoice must be verified; and the purchase order journal record must be updated. As ordered items are received, they must be checked against the purchase order for both quantity and quality; the prices, terms, and discounts on the invoice must be verified; and the purchase order journal record must be updated.

The size of the purchase order file will of course

depend upon the number of outstanding order at any one time, the number of line items on each order, and the number of invoices. Representative figures might be: 1000 outstanding invoices, 5 line items each, and 2 shipments each. Under such conditions, the file would contain about 328,000 characters.

Accounts payable. The function of the "accounts payable module" is to handle the actual payments to vendors, and maintain records for the cumulative status of vendor accounts. The basic file is the set of vendor records. The sources of data include purchase orders, vouchers (i.e., forms which substantiate financial liability and confirm receipt of material), cash disbursement and "credit received" records, past cumulative records, and other history.

Reports can be produced showing the status of each vendor's account. Again, "exception criteria" can be used to highlight vendors representing one or another kind of problem. Reports on cash disbursements and cash requirements can be produced to aid management in financial planning.

The size of the account payable file depends upon the number of vendors, the number of orders and invoices, and the number of payments. With 1000 vendors, each with an average for a year's historical record of 10 orders, 20 invoices, and payments, the file would contain 900,000 characters.

Parameters for estimation

Each of the three financial files we have discussed is relatively small. (The bookkeeping file might be as large as 165,000 characters; the purchase order file, 330,000 characters; and the accounts payable file, 900,000 characters). File creation (conversion) therefore represents a minor consideration in evaluating the work load. File interrogation is primarily handled through the use of printed reports. Maintenance and reporting are therefore the primary considerations in evaluating the work load. For each of these two file management functions, processing time estimates must be developed. The processing load is primarily determined by the number of financial transactions and file record reports each month and the processing time required for each.

Estimates of keypunching time and input. The data for financial processing comes primarily from data required for other operations, and therefore it is assumed that the keypunching and input will have been done as part of them.

Estimates of sorting time. The nature of financial accounting does-not require high-speed on-line access, so batch processing once a week should be completely adequate. To do so efficiently with large-scale computers usually involves sorting transactions into order by the identification of file records affected (budgetary account, purchase order number, vendor number); frequently, a given transaction affecting several files will be sorted two or three times. For the small-scale computer system, the sorting times are usually so great that direct-access processing may be more efficient.

Sorting is also required as part of the preparation of reports. The time to do so is determined by the number of file records to be included in each sort. For purposes of estimation, it might be assumed that every file record will appear in at least one weekly report.

Estimates of file access. Given the sizes of the three financial files, the only remaining issue in estimating file access is the frequency of file up-date (which might be assumed as weekly), since this determines the batch size in file searching.

Estimates of computing. In general, a given transaction will affect at least one record in each of the three financial files. It could therefore be estimated that about three file update operations, will be required per transaction. During reporting, each file record will affect several subtotals.

Estimates of output. Transactions which affect file records usually result in some form of output-a check, an error report, an instruction to staff personnel, etc.- about one line of printed output per transaction. For file reporting, the estimates is two lines of printed output per file record, each reporting period.

Estimates of traffic load. The crucial issues are the number of financial transactions, VT, to be handled each month and the number of file records, VR, to be reported on. If each file record is reported on each week, then VR would be four times the number of actual file records.

Personnel data processing

Regulations, procedures, records, and other aspects of data processing are as necessary in personnel management as in other parts of library management.

All libraries must have personnel information centralised, confidential, and adequate for efficient operation. The administrative forms include, for example:

1. Employment applications, including personal history records;
2. References and interview reports.
3. Changes of status, vacations, leaves of absence.
4. Service reports.

The payroll forms include, for example:

1. Payroll records.
2. Checks.
3. Payroll reports.

Of course, administrative records are usually stored in personnel dossiers in their original form. However, a good deal of the information recorded on them could be effectively utilised if stored on magnetic tape files: Listings of personnel can be prepared for a great variety of purposes; identification of those with specialised skills can be aided through computer processing; statistical analyses of the characteristics of different categories of personnel can be easily produced; and necessary personnel actions can be automatically generated.

The personnel data processing subsystem therefore should include all of the functions necessary for maintaining personnel records, displaying available resources, predicting future personnel needs, and reporting as required both by library management and by administrative departments within the parent institution. It should provide all of the necessary time-keeping functions for all categories of library employees. The system should provide on demand or in regular periodic reports information necessary for making a variety of personnel decisions. It should provide statistical summaries of data describing in meaningful ways the character of the library work force and its distribution within the library.

Most of the functions can be designed to occur at regular periodic intervals. However, it is anticipated that there will be occasional needs for special summary reports prepared from the up-to-date files.

Management data processing

General nature

Cost accounting. The objectives of cost accounting are to provide reports of the cost of each process and job order in the library. These would include comparisons of actual costs with standard costs and reports on the efficiency of each department.

The sources of data in a cost accounting system include employee payroll data, employee job tickets, and standard cost and time data. For each employees, production records must be maintained, usually daily. The files are usually historical and standard cost data. The reporting function is the basic one.

Production control. The objective of production control is to schedule work efficiently through technical processing. The sources of data include forecasts of services required (as derived from past statistics, management acquisition plans, etc.), standard times for technical processing steps, statistics on existing backlogs and work loads, and decision rules for determining production schedules.

Forms and files

We presented some typical records for cost accounting data-both manual and punched card. These represent the basic source of data for both cost accounting and production control.

Estimates of work load

The work load in management data processing is basically a function of the size of the library staff: The input for cost accounting requires the conversion of production and time data for each staff member; production control involves the printout of management data for each staff member.

Estimates of keypunching and input. Each day, each employee would record time data on cost accounting sheets. Many employees are on tasks covered by "process-costing", and for them the data can be obtained from prepunched time cards; for those on tasks covered by "job-costing", it might mean five or ten lines of data each day. The bulk of employees are likely to be involved in process-costed work, and the keypunching task therefore is likely to average about 50 characters per employee per day.

7

FINANCIAL MANAGEMENT

Finance underpins all organisational activities. It enables staff to be employed, technology to be applied, buildings to be erected, equipment to be bought, services to be provided. If an organisation cannot acquire adequate finance, or does not use its finance efficiently and effectively, it will fail to meet its objectives. Financial management is thus an integral part of each element in the 'management cycle' of planning, implementing, and control. In order to be implemented, policies and objectives have to be translated into plans or programmes for action. Central to that planning process is an assessment of the resources that will be needed in order to accomplish the plan, and a calculation of the cost of those resources. By calculating costs and setting these against the benefits which are expected as the outcome of the plan, and the placing this cost-benefit analysis in the wider context of the organisation's objectives and overall financial position, it becomes possible to rank plans and programmes into priority order, to set financial timescales for major projects, and to allocate resources accordingly.

As plans are implemented, financial considerations become a crucial part of the 'control' function of management. Estimations will have been made regarding income that the organisation is likely to receive and expenditure that will be incurred. Management needs to keep a close watch on the relationship between actual income and expenditure on which plans, programmes and timescales will have been based. On a day-to-day basis, this is usually done through the budgeting process. Each department within the organisation has a budget which sets limits on expenditure and it is the responsibility of departmental management to see that expenditure is kept within those limits. Similarly, each department may have targets for income, and performance will be monitored in relation to those targets.

As well as the continuous process of control through budget management, organisations and departments will also, from time to time, be subject to audit, by which the financial control system and other associated aspects of management performance are scrutinised. Auditors may be internal or external to the organisation and may either limit themselves to comment on the organisation's accounting processes and financial management, or may be given a wider remit to conduct a 'management, audit which explores all aspects of management performance. In the UK, for example, the role of the Audit Commission is to ensure that local authorities and public bodies comply with law and good practice in their financial control, and also to see that they show 'economy, efficiency and effectiveness' in the use of resources to deliver services.

Control is also exercised through an organisation's accountability to its owners or to those responsible for its governance. A commercial organisation will produce an annual report containing various audited financial statements (such as a profit and loss account for the year under review, and a balance sheet which sets assets against liabilities). This will be presented at an annual general meeting of—in the case of a publicly quoted company—the shareholders. In the commercial world, these figures provide the ultimate control mechanism. Their analysis will determine the level of confidence in the company's prospects and that level of confidence will determine the company's share price and ability to raise money in the various financial markets.

A similar process, although without the regulating mechanisms of the money markets, applies to organisations which are not in the commercial sector. An annual report, containing statements of income and expenditure, will be presented at some form of annual general meeting. Confidence in the organisation's management and prospect will be determined, largely, by analysing these figures in relation to the 'estimates' for that year or the corresponding figures for previous years.

Strong financial planning and control, then, is vital to an organisation's future prospects, and a critical factor in determining the level of confidence which those with a 'stake' in the organisation (as part of its ownership or governance) have in its management. This is particularly so at a time when economic constraints are increasing the pressure on management to account for the ways in which resources are used and to seek out new ways by which income might be generated. In many organisations-most noticeably in the non-commercial public sector-traditional approaches to financial management are changing to reflect this need to demonstrate accountability and 'enterpreneurialism' or enterprise.

The financial context

The process of financial analysis, planning, and control operates on three levels:

- the external environments of legislation, audit, the economy, and the money markets; issues of company law, taxation, etc.; strategies for investment and raising finance.
- the organisation's assets and liabilities: management of current and fixed assets, and of short-term and long-term liabilities; matters such as the capital 'gearing'—that is, the ratio of debt (funds raised by borrowing) to equity (funds raised through shareholding)—of a company.
- budget management (using planned limits on expenditure and targets for income) at departmental level.

The library manager is involved, primarily, with the third-departmental-level of financial management. The library is unlikely to be, of itself, a corporate entity; it is more likely to be a department within a larger organisation. Matters to do with external financial environments or the overall management of assets and liabilities are likely to be the concern of a separate department specifically concerned with financial matters. Financial resources are available to the library, but are not actually held in the library (other than relatively insignificant sums of 'petty cash' or a 'float' of small change in the till). When the library spends money, it does not do so directly. The usual practice (in the UK) is to 'raise an official order' authorising payment which is then passed to the finance department for action. Similarly when the library receives money it does so on behalf of its parent organisation. It is the organisation (not the library itself) which issues invoices and to which cheques are payable. Cash income (from fines and fees) is passed on, by the library, to the finance department to be administered.

This process does have potential inefficiencies and difficulties, the bureaucracy of an 'official order' is unacceptable to some potential suppliers, particularly those small 'alternative' or 'radical' bookshops which can provide important material from minority publishers. It also becomes difficult for the library to take advantage of any cash-with-order discounts. Cash management strategies are out of the library's hands: with no control over when accounts are paid, the library may not be able to benefit from the fast-payment discounts which are sometimes offered by suppliers and publishers. If all income is passed to a central administrative unit, it becomes difficult to ensure that income generated by the library service is actually credited to the library's budget.

There are some instances when the wider financial world of asset/liability management and external economic environments has a direct impact on library management; for example, when an organisation has to cut back on expenditure because external economic factors have led to a shortfall in projected income. This has happened in a large number of commercial organisations on both sides of the Atlantic where financial management in a time of recession has led to cutbacks in corporate overheads—often including a significant reduction in resourcing for the company's library or information unit. Dealing with 'the cuts' has also become a commonplace of financial management in UK public sector libraries as a result of the government's policy of reducing public expenditure; and this experience may well mirrored in the USA as government gets to grips with the Federal budget deficit.

Pressure from central government to reduce expenditure and determination by local government, in some places, to oppose this policy and maintain or improve levels of service has produced a liquidity crisis in some UK local authorities. Current assets (i.e. those which can be quickly converted into cash) are not sufficient to meet short-term liabilities. A number of local authorities, faced with this situation, have decided to improve liquidity by converting fixed assets (such as buildings) into cash by a process of sale and lease-back. Some public library services have found their buildings converted into capital assets and 'cashed' in this way. However, on the whole, library managers tend to be concerned with the day-to-day operation of budgets and financial reporting systems rather than the strategies levels of financial management to do with assets, liabilities and the economic environment.

Thus, a commercial organisation will produce a balance sheet (setting assets against liabilities) and a profit and loss account (setting income against expenditure) which will be subjected to a process of 'ratio analysis" in order to assess that organisation's liquidity (ability to meet short-term obligations), asset management (ability to convert assets into income), debt management (ability to meet long-term debts), and profitability. This type of statement and analysis is not usually appropriate for a library, unless it operates as a corporate entity. The library is more likely to be a single departmental budget centre within the organisation. It is also likely to be regarded as, primarily, a spending rather than income-generating department. In commercial organisations, the library is usually regarded as part of the corporate 'overhead'—that is, the costs incurred centrally in order to support the company's activities. The year-end figures for the library-as-department (in both public and private sectors) are likely to show expenditure and then income (to give a 'bottom line' figure for net expenditure) itemised under a number of budget headings, such as those used in the CIPFA public library statistics (expenditure on staff, bookstock, etc.; income from fines and fees, hirings, etc.).

Comparing these tow types of financial statement indicates two important difference of approach. The structure and emphasis of the commercial organisation's accounts focus on profit (income less costs equals net surplus), while a library's accounts, traditionally, focus on expenditure (costs less income equals net spending).

When a commercial organisation's figure are itemised in detail for internal management purposes, a separate set of figures is often produced for each product. It is thus possible to monitor the performance of each product in terms of income generated and costs incurred. The library's figures are detailed under budget heading itemising different types of income source and spending area. It is not usually possible, from the structure of these figures, to identify income generated and costs incurred by individual 'products' or services.

These distinctions reflect the traditional differences between a business and a service approach. It is important for a business to focus on profit and the financial performance of individual produces; output and outcomes are expressed in financial terms. For service organisations, operating as part of the corporate overhead or supported by public funding, the focus is on efficient deployment of resources. Inputs are subject to financial control and scrutiny. Outputs and outcomes are expressed by usage data and satisfaction levels; not primarily in financial terms.

However, some elements of the 'business' approach to financial management are beginning to be applied to library service. The library manager's financial responsibility has been limited, traditionally, to the budgeting process and specifically to the control of an expenditure budget. However, this responsibility is widening as a result of the pressure for accountability and enterprise, linked to the move, in many organisations, to devolve service unit. Library managers are now involved in:

- income generation: the library is no longer regarded simply as an 'overhead'. In 'closed' communities (such as universities or commercial organisations) the library may 'sell' its services of other departments within the organisation, or individual departments allocate resources to the library rather than the library's budget coming from a central fund. In 'open' communities like those served by the public library, the pressure is to diversify the resource base, reducing dependence on centrally allocated funds. In both cases, there is an attempt to express one aspect of performance in terms of income received.
- costing; analysing costs in detail-often at the level of unit cost (that is, the full cost, in detail, of a single process or action)—in order to apportion expenditure to specific areas of activity. It thus becomes possible to produce figures for library activities which equate to the 'cost of sale' figures produced, in business, for individual products.
- performance budgeting: financial statements which express performance by setting income against costs. These become appropriate if the library is operating a service on a self-funding basis (by which income from the service pays for the costs of that service) or with the intention of generating additional net income.

In these ways, libraries-even the public sector-are no longer seen simply as 'part of the overhead' or as a spending department granted a budget from centrally deployed resources. Rather, they become 'cost centres'. Costs (and income) are disaggregated and apportioned to individual 'cost units'—service point, functional departments (e.g. acquisitions, cataloguing, inter-lending), service programmes (e.g. user education programmes, events for children, public library 'out-reach' programmes). It thus becomes possible to relate costs to perceived benefits in a more precise way.

Public sector libraries in the UK are being encouraged by government to explore the possibilities for 'joint ventures' with private-sector businesses, and to investigate the potential for contracting out aspects of library service to competitive tender. The first—if not yet the second—of these is also becoming a feature of library service planning in the USA. Both these moves accentuate the need for precise statements of units costs and service outcomes.

The library budget

To coordinate financial management across the library system two subsystems are needed:

- a reporting/accounting system; to deal with the flow of money into (fines, fees, etc.) and out of (stock purchases, etc.) the library; and to monitor that flow.
- a budgeting system: to estimate future income and expenditure (planning), and to monitor actual figures so that variations from the estimates can be identified and investigated (control).

These subsystems are linked to the organisational hierarchy by the process of authorising expenditure. The authority to spent should be clearly defined (in terms of budget areas and cash limits) and line managers given that authority should also take on responsibility for regulating their spending so that it falls within the authorised budget limits. So, for example, a branch librarian in a public library or a subject librarian in an academic library may be given authority/responsibility for a portion of the money to be spent on stock.

The budgeting cycle begins with the process of estimating expenditure under two general headings:

- 'revenue' or 'recurrent' expenditure; that is, all day-to-day operating expenses, staff salaries and other costs, spending on library stock etc.
- 'capital expenditure; that is, major non-recurrent items of expenditure such as the cost of building or refurbishing a library, buying a new vehicle, upgrading the computer system, etc.

There is a measure of overlap in that 'capital 'expenditure may have 'revenue' implications (for example, buying a new mobile library may mean employing additional staff), or, if capital expenditure is funded by borrowing, there will be recurrent debt charges. But, in general, organisations tend to treat the revenue budget and the capital programme as two separate items for consideration and decision-making.

On a day-to-day basis, library managers are less concerned with the capital programme than with the revenue budget. Capital expenditure accounts for around 6.6% of overall expenditure in both public and university libraries in UK. The traditional library budget for revenue expenditure had four key features:

- It is 'historical' with estimated for the next year based largely on expenditure in preceding years.

- It is a 'line' budget, dividing expenditure into broad categories (staff, books, etc.).
- It operates on a yearly cycle, with no carry-over from one year to the next.
- It is subject to time lag, with estimates calculated a considerable period in advance of actual expenditure.

All four of these features can cause difficulties. 'Historical' budgeting-because it is based on past precedents and not future objectives—tends to reinforce the status quo and inhibit radical change. A 'line' budget makes it difficult to use anything other than a historical base for estimates, and can also limit the library manager's financial flexibility; 'virement' (that is, the authority to move funds from one budget heading to another) is usually strictly limited.

The yearly cycle imposes artificial constraints which can affect spending decisions. Any money left in the budget at the end of the accounting year will be 'clawed back' by the parent organisation, rather than carried over for the library's use. There is thus pressure on the library manager to spend up to budget limits—and many library suppliers can tell stories of librarians on minor spending sprees in February and March, emptying the book fund before the close of the financial year.

The time lag between estimates and actual expenditure means that the budget is affected by inflation which, over time, reduces the real value of money. A budget may show an increase, in cash terms, over the previous year's figures. But if that increase is less than the rate of inflation, then the budget will have been reduced in real terms, that is in terms of actual spending power. In some instances inflation allowances are added to the budget (for example, to met increased staff costs resulting from a pay award). However, inflation allowances do not always cover the real increased cost. The price of books, for example consistently rises faster than the 'rate of inflation' so an inflation allowance based on RPI and added to the bookfund would mean a reduction, in real terms, of spending power to buy books. It is often the case that budgets are 'cash limited'—that is, no further additional allowances can be made and any increased costs have to be met within the existing budget limits.

There have been some attempts to move away from 'historical' and 'line' budgets to a process of budgeting based on activities and priorities. 'Zero-based' budgeting disregards historical precedent and begins with the financial equivalent of a 'blank sheet of paper' so that each area of expenditure has to be justified a new at the start of the planning and estimating process. 'Performance' budgeting is based on individual areas of activity and service, including calculating the costs of that activity. Both seem attractive in theory—linking the estimating/budgeting processes more closely to the process of determining service priorities and monitoring service performance—but both are complex and time-consuming to put into practice.

When library budgets are broken down into component parts, a clear pattern emerges which is common for all types of library. David Liddle offers the following indicative breakdown for 'a fairly typical public library service' in the UK.

Staffing costs, salaries, wages and on costs	56%
Building costs, heat, light, rates, repairs, painting, debt charges, central charges	23%

Library materials, books, records, newspapers, etc.	18%
Running costs, printing, stationery, furniture, etc.	3%

James Thompson and Reg Carr suggest that UK university library budgets break down roughly as follows:

Staff	555
Acquisitions	35%
Binding	4%
Sundries	6%

For may librarians, financial management will mean management of all or a portion of the acquisitions budget. This, in itself, poses interesting questions. In the public library context, should each branch be given a fixed 'slice' to spend and manage, or should the fund be retained centrally, with each branch bidding for money in the light of stock selection decisions made by branch staff? Many public library systems operate the former practice (and thus give line mangers some useful experience of budgeting at an early stage in their careers), although Liddle seems to advocate the latter practices in stressing that stock selection should be kept separate from budget management:

> Many systems confuse the selection process with the essential budget monitoring process which must ensure that the budget is balanced to enable phased spending throughout the year. The budget monitoring process should be separate from the professional job of selection. Professional judgment should not be distorted by the availability or lack of money to spend. Librarians must select what they need. Whether or not they have it depends upon the person whose responsibility it is to control the budget.

In the academic library context, how should the library manager apportion funds for stock purchase between academic departments? Whatever simple or complex formula is adopted (student numbers, academic level of work, 'library-intensity' of courses, average cost of titles, useful shelf-life of knowledge, etc.), there will be complaints from departments which feel hard done by. At Birmingham polytechnic, partly to alleviate this problem and partly to reduce central overheads and apportion expenditure to individual 'cost centres,' the faculties are each given a national amount for the library as part of their operating budget and they can then chose the actual amount they wish to spend on library stock. A proportion of what would have been the library's acquisitions budget has been, in effect, taken away from the library manger's control and handed over to the customer. It is that customer who then determines what amount will be spent on library stock as competing claims on the faculty's resource are reconciled.

Managing the book fund means dealing with, library suppliers—commercial businesses which supply and process library stock to order. Because librarianship is a relatively small world, because many specialist suppliers employ professional librarians and show a genuine interest in issue of current concern, and because of the annual round of professional conferences attended by both librarians and ' the trade', a cosy and quite personal relationship can build up between library managers and the suppliers with whom they deal. Because of the Net Book Agreement (which fixes book prices and offers a standard discount for libraries), suppliers in the UK cannot compete of price. However, they can and do compete on performance-speed of supply, quality and variety of stock processing, bibliographic support stock selection.

It is, of course, the library manager's responsibility to make supply decisions on the basis of careful cost/benefit analysis.

The difficulties which library managers can experience in subdividing the acquisitions budget should give librarians some empathy with the difficulties experienced by the parent organisation in allocating the overall budget between competing claimants, including the library. One of the important functions of the library's senior management is to acquire funds for the library by influencing decision-making in those arenas where the organisation's total 'cake' is subdivided into individual 'slices'.

The amount of money spent on libraries may seem large, but in most organisations the library budget is, in fact, a very small part of the overall budget. Liddle suggests that public library spending accounts fc just 1.5 per cent to 2.5 per cent of total expenditure in those UK local authorities which are responsible for an education service, and around 5 per cent of total expenditure in non-education authorities. In UK universities and polytechnics, the library account for 4 per cent of 4.5 per cent of total expenditure.

The relatively small size of these budgets can have advantages and disadvantages. On the one hand, the library service can be seen as relatively cheap and the therefore as 'good value' for money: the Chief Executive of the UK Library Association is fond of noting that the public library service costs less than 'half a bar of chocolate' per person per week. It may also be the case that when a cut is needed in the overall budget, the library is left alone because a proportionate reduction in library spending would not produce any great saving in cash terms.

On the other hand, an 'across the board' cut in all budgets within the organisation can have a disproportionately damaging effect on a department, like the library, which has only a small budget with which to work. It may also be difficult to get senior management within the parent organisation to pay sufficient attention to library matters when the library's budget represents activity. An education department may spend close to half of all the money spent by a UK local authority. If the Education committee deals also with the library service (which spends between one per cent and two per cent of the authority's total expenditure), how much time will be given to library matters?

The amount of money given to libraries by their parent organisation varies widely even amongst comparable institution. In part, this may well relate to the character and quality of library management. Research into public libraries and their place within local authority structures has concluded that the nature and development of the service depends less on the organisational framework and more on the qualities of the Chief Librarian. This reinforces the point that library managers need to get involved in decision-making at the organisational level and promote the value of investment in the library.

Investment decisions are based on the perceived return, or 'pay back', on that investment. That return may be in the form of actual income or some other tangible benefit, or some less visible but equally attractive outcome. The outcomes from library service are more likely to be 'invisible earnings' than tangible returns, and for this reason, it is particularly important for the library's senior management to be aware of the political dimension of organisational decision-making. Library management can then use this dimension in stressing the payback on investments made in the library service. An academic institution, for example, might be interested in the library's contribution to student-centered learning (and a more efficient staff student ratio). One local authority might be attached by the library's potential to provide information support to local businesses; another by the library's potential to help redress disadvantage. A commercial corporation might be swayed by the idea that information provided by the library can contribute to competitive advantage. In each case, the library's senior management must find the appropriate 'political' argument by which to advance the library's case for adequate resources.

Faced with constraints on funds granted to the library by its parent organisation, and with political pressure to be more entrepreneurial and less dependent on such granted funds, many library managers are seeking other sources of income. There are basically three types of alternative income source:

- grants from external funds: for example, public libraries in the UK have benefited from funding provided by the Manpower Services Commission, the Home Office, the various Arts Associations, the European Commission, and so on.
- trading activities (for example, a library shop or publishing programme), including joint ventures between public-sector libraries and private-sector business.
- charging for library service: for example (as the UK green paper on public library financing suggests) defining the 'basic' service, and levying a direct charge on customers using any 'additional' or 'specialised' service.

A discussion on the philosophical/ethical/political issues surrounding the 'fee, or free? Debate is beyond the scope of this book-except to note that library managers need to confront these issues and build them into the policy-making process. Of relevance here are the practical implications for library financial management of trading, charging, and the use of externally granted funds.

A key distinction between trading/charging activities and traditional library budgeting is that the latter is based on a fixed income (the eventual budget allocation for the year) while trading and charging imply that income will be variable, depending on the volume and price of services and products sold. Library managers may need to learn financial techniques designed to manage variable income and ensure that income is sufficient to meet expenditure.

For trading operations which are separated financially from the 'basic' library service, it may be necessary to prepare a cashflow budget. This itemises estimated income and expenditure (usually on a month-by-month basis, projected forward for a year) in order to indicate net cash flow and ensure that the operation has enough cash in hand to cover its immediate liabilities. It may also be necessary, in pricing products and services, to us break-even analysis in order to determine the point at which a particular activity will cover its costs. To take the practical example of a library's publishing programme:

- A particular book incurs £1,000 in fixed costs (for example, cost of staff, building, etc.) and £5 per unit in variable costs (costs which vary with the volume of sales such as author's royalties or the unit cost of printing and distribution), assuming a sale of 200 copies. Given a selling price of £10 each, a simple calculation indicates that if all 200 copies are sold the operation will break even.

$$\frac{\text{Fixed operating costs}}{(\text{sale price per unit}) - (\text{variable cost per unit})}$$

$$\frac{1000}{(10 - 5)} \qquad \frac{1000}{5} = 200$$

This is simplistic example, but it shows that careful analysis of fixed and variable costs, and finely judged decisions regarding price and likely volume of sales, are needed if library managers are to be successful as 'retailers' of products and services.

An important element in many of the processes described above is costing. The analysis of costs is central to: break-even services; making cashflow budgeting; deliberations on charging for services; making the case for resources within the parent organisation by demonstrating 'value for money'; choosing commercial suppliers; establishing joint ventures between public-sector libraries and private-sector business; the process of estimating likely expenditure; the development of any form of 'performance' budgeting.

The CIPFA report, referring to public libraries, suggests that cost management has not been developed in the past because requirements for public accountability have not been so pressing. Library managers have tended to work with subjective and qualitative considerations more than objective measures, and no tradition has been built up of financial or managerial accountability. This is changing, and the report suggests that a costing system will enable library managers to:

- relate priority shifts to costs;
- develop more meaningful pricing policies;
- demonstrate exactly how much money is being spent on what services.

The models developed by CIPFA and the ALA enable costs to be allocated to cost centres (that is, individual service points or support sections) and analysed by functional areas (that is, areas of service or support that cut across centres, such as 'reference service' or 'publicity'). CIPFA also explored the possibility of determining costs in relation to individual 'clients groups' and the report recommends further research into this approach.

There is strong current interest in the UK in the development of a 'cost centre' approach to the financial management of library service. Traditionally, the line manger of a service unit has responsibility for a portion of the stock budget while most of the major costs associated with the units are dealt with centrally by middle/senior management. A 'cost centre' approach would disaggregate central costs as much as possible, apportioning spending on staff, buildings, supplies, etc. to each service unit. Financial management (including decisions regarding local virement and the proportional expenditure on staff, stock, supplies, etc.) could then be devolved to the line manager of each service unit. The approach has already been implemented with regard to state- funded schools in the UK which are becoming largely autonomous in terms of financial management.

The CIPFA report points out that libraries do not have easily definable products or outputs which can be quantified, and that there is usually little financial expertise available within the library department itself. However it is a clear indication of the move towards a more precise accounting of costs in relation to activities—whether those activities are defined in terms of service points, support sections, functional areas, or customer groups.

A distinction can be drawn, then, between the traditional approach to library resourcing-with the library dependent for funds on its parent organisation, and the budget related to previous expenditure—and the 'entrepreneurial' or 'enterprise' by diversifying sources of income, makes the library more self reliant and less dependent on its parent organisation. The characteristics of this approach are clear:

- 'Value for money': analysing and allocating costs, identifying outputs, and reviewing performance.
- 'Cost centres': developing financial management to the level of individual service units.
- Competitive tendering; based on the proposition that it may, sometimes, be more efficient to contract out a particular activity, enabling it to take place without directly providing it. Thus the client (for example, a library service) specifies costs, standards and targets for the activity being contracted out, and then monitors the contractor's performance.
- Alternative funding strategies: attracting external funds, developing trading activities (including joint ventures), and charging for certain services.

Applying this approach may not make a considerable difference to libraries in purely financial terms. Library income is small in relation to expenditure and this will remain the case for the great majority of libraries. CIPFA figures (for 1985/6) show that, in England, public library income (£21.6m) covered just

5.2% of expenditure (£413.4m). If the notional target of £50m income, given in the UK government's green paper, were reached, this would still cover only 12% of the present level of expenditure. Most libraries will continue to remain, more ore less, dependent on the budget granted to them by their parent organisation.

But the size of that grant-the library's 'slice' of the organisational 'cake'—may well depend, in part, on the parent organisation's perception of financial management within the library department. Library managers need to be able to present a strong and politically astute case for library resourcing. They need to prove that they can handle, creatively and successfully, the difficult operational decisions that follows when the allocated budget does not meet the estimates put forward. They need to demonstrate enterprise and accountability in their approach to financial management. They may then find it easier to convince those responsible for policy and resources that investment in the library service represents good value for money.

8

LIBRARY RECORDS

It is natural for an organisation to record information about the various activities of its different organs to that it can judge their working with precision and ease. A library being a public institution must maintain records of its essential services and departments so that it can place before its patrons authentic information when required. "In order to describe the performance and measure the success of his organisation, it is necessary or the Librarian to have available significant and complete records of resources."[1] "Such records may help to show the accomplishments of the library, costs of its services, and the short-comings in its organisation."[2] So the records are maintained not for records' sake only but these have set purposes behind them.

The word 'Record' means 'to write something in such a manner that it is available in a permanent form and that it has a lasting value'. To give it the real value, the information regarding the activities of a library, which have a permanent value, should be recorded on such writing materials which are capable of standing the test of time due to it being put to constant use. The traditional form of a such material has been the bound register but now the shift towards card form is significant.

A research scholar attempting to write the history of an institution must seek for an authoritative, authentic and factual information. It can be available in the registers maintained by the concerned institution. The records contain the original information whereas statistics, though, generally based on these records, can be distorted in a desired direction but the records are difficult to be mutilated. So, it is all the more essential to maintain such reliable records in order to vouchsafe the availability of trustworthy information.

The library records can facilitate the work of the Library Committee for ascertaining as to whether the amount sanctioned for the maintenance of the library has been properly utilised or not. The taxpayer also can be satisfied only through factual records. The Librarian can present his point of view to the Library Authority by taking help of the factual records. If the Library Authority doubts the manipulation of statistics, it can be easily satisfied by one corroboration of the information by the production of the original records.

Kinds of records

It is quile reasonable and proper that we maintain records about books and equipment, the readers and services-technical and readers's services. These may be better classified as:-

(i) Records of books and other non-book resources available in the library;

(ii) Cost records i.e. total cost and unit cost, etc.;

(iii) Service records i.e. services rendered by the library;' and

(iv) Administrative records.

Records of books

The books which are acquired in the library are meant for use of one and all the readers of the locality or the institution, as the case may be. They funds for their acquisition come from the public exchequer and it is essential to justify the expenditure of each penny. To satisfy the auditors who serve as checks and balances against the executive action, the office must record everything which has cost the exchequer, otherwise there is danger or wastage of money.

Books are meant for use of one and all and if any reader damages or loses the books of the library, the library record should help in ascertaining the actual cost price of the lost book which is to be realised from the defaulter reader or he may be guided as to wherefrom he can procure a new copy and replace the lost book. In the absence of such records, it would be well-nigh impossible to have the accurate information and there may arise many disputes as to the price, edition etc. of the lost book.

For this purpose, it is customary with the libraries to maintain a Accession Register, the specimen which is given below:

Date	Accession No.	Author	Title	Publisher and Place of Publication	Price	Vol.	Collation	Binding	Source of supply	Bill No.	Date and Amt.	Call No.	Remarks

Of late, a new school which may be called 'the Utilitarian School' has started thinking in terms of utility which may be derived from certain procedures and practices. The protagonists of this school compare the relative advantages and disadvantages and prefer to introduce those practices which are advantageous without sacrificing the essential features. The modern method of keeping a record of books is the conversion of the Book Selection Card into an Accession card after it has served the purpose of book selection and book order. It saves time, labour and money which, they say, might be otherwise wasted in preparing a separate record.

Records of non-book materials

For non-book reading materials i.e. films, micro-films, micro-cards, micro-fiche maps, atlases, gramophone records etc. a type of Accession Register may be useful but additional columns for detailed information about the script, format, and other physical aspects should be provided which are not found in records of reading materials in book from. But it is advisable to maintain separate registers for non-book materials since their purpose, use, handling and location etc. will otherwise bring in so many difficulties.

The Utilitarians would prefer to keep the records of these non-book materials also on cards.

Account books

Another important record relating to the acquisition of books etc. is the maintenance of detailed information about the allocation of book funds for various departments or subjects and preserving the relevant bills so that the library authority may be able to satisfy itself that the book fund has bee properly utilised. This is also essential to avoid double payments.

Specimen of an allocation register

This register may be ledger type and a few pages may be allotted to each department or subject:

Name of the Dept./Subject......total Amount Sanctioned

Name and Head of the Grant............................

Sr. No.	Bill No. and Date	Name of the supplier	Amount of the Bill	Deduction, if any	Total Amount of the Bill	Total Grant of the Dept.	Balance available	Remarks

Specimen of a bill register

The Bill Files may be kept either supplier-wise or subjective-wise. The files are to be kept in vertical files cabinets in an alphabetical order and the bills are to be arranged date-wise so that any bill may be located at any moment without loss of time. This can be done by keeping the duplicate or triplicate copy of the bill, as the case may be.

Shelf list

The next important record of books is the maintenance of the Shelf Register or List. Prior to the introduction of cards, the Shelf List was maintained in a register and later on in loose leaf form since the former lacked mobility and elasticity. In order to enable the insertion of entries, which have to be interpolated continuously, the register of loose-leaf kind failed. The registers became cumbersome and voluminous and lacked neatness and clarity. The latest accepted method is to keep the shelf list on cards. The cards are kept in cabinets and are arranged in a classified order. The utility of this record lies in the fact that it can show the position of any book on the shelves i.e., it generally gives the location number, if some departure from the classified order is practised in shelving the books. The shelf list is the most handy and time-saving tool for stock-verification purposes since each card represents exactly each book in the same position as it is to be found on the shelves.

Book catalogue

Another important library record for books is the provision of catalogue of books. It becomes instrumental in helping the readers in finding out their required materials whether they approach the books through their author, subject or title. It also saves the time of the reference assistants since it is an easy key to the library book stock.

The catalogue, which is now generally maintained on cards, was, in the past (some national and bigger libraries even now prefer to have printed catalogues) got Printed. The former is decidely better for general libraries.

Technical records

The most important records which are maintained in the technical Section of a library pertain to the adoption of certain modified practices in classification and cataloguing procedures.

A staff Manual is an essential and impersonal record so that any technical hand can know the modifications intrcduced in the classification and cataloguing procedures. It would be better if these amendments are recorded in a classified manner and many copies of the manual are made available for the use of the staff members.

Similarly, a Name Authority File is essential so that every person in the Technical Section may work with consistency and may use the adopted names without any departure.

Cost records

The cost records include the total amount spent on staff, book purchase, their preparation, their issuing to the readers and the techniques involved in their preservation. In short, the cost records reveal the total cost of providing library service during a particulars period by taking into account all the amounts spent from the moment the books are selected to the time these are actually made available to the readers. From these records, we can arrive at the unit cost through cost-accounting. This information is very useful to know the desirability or otherwise of a library service. Records can prove easily as to whether all these routines are worthwhile or not. These records can be kept separately under the following separate heads of account:

1. Salaries and wages.
2. Purchase of and other reading materials.
3. Library binding, etc.
4. Maintenance charges of the building.
5. Heating, cooling and other charges.
6 Miscellaneous.

The population figures and the number of readers or users of the library must be handy for doing the exact cost-accounting.

Service records

The service records are essential for those departments of the library with which, the public or the readers have a direct connection. It is very essential to have perfect record of the dealings with the public. These stand in good stead in difficult times and can serve the purpose of an authentic index of the usefulness or otherwise of a library to the community or the institution.

Visitors' register

A visitors' register is essential to know the interest the inhabitants of a particular locality take in using the library resources.

We can judge from these records as to whether the community is utilising the library resources properly or not. It is a daily record of visitors who visit library. We can see whether the library is popular amongst its patrons or not.

Specimen of visitors' register

Date	Sr. No.	Name of visitor	Address	Occupation	Purpose of visit	Remarks

Issue records

Certain records are maintained by the Lending Section, which is generally the busiest Section of a library. The Issue Counter is the place from where the reading material is issued to the readers for a limited time so that the other readers may also borrow the same material on a later date. From this premises we can conclude that the following records are necessary at the Issue counter:

1. *Reader's record*—the names and addresses of the readers.

2. Time record—the period for which the books are issued.
3. Book record—the clue giving information as to which book is issued out.

Readers' record

In small libraries, the readers' record is maintained in a register and the registration of readers as members is recorded in seriatum in a ruled register in which the name, address, occupation and the class of readers are noted. But big libraries have to adopt some such method which enables the staff members to locate the requisite information without loss of time. Registration Cards File arranged in an alphabetical or classified order is the most practised method.

Advanced countries like U.S.A. and Great Britain have started using Visadex made by Demco and Remington Rand Co. it is possible to see at a glance hundreds of names of the readers within a second. Similarly, we find in banks also that they have got specimen signature cards which are wither arranged alphabetically or according to the allotted serial numbers. It is very simple and time-saving. Libraries must keep such records so that in case of dispute, the matter can be solved by having resort to the original registration records. These records are essential to know as to whom a particular book has been issued, and if necessity arises, the books can be recalled from the readers.

Time record

As already explained, the books are meant not for chosen few only out for one and all. The resources of a library being limited, we have to put a time limit for keeping the books for home use so that every reader gets a chance to make use of the reading material. It is found from experience that if no limits is placed on the issuing of books most of the books will be lying idle at borrowers' homes and the very aim of books and libraries will be defeated.

A order to know the date on which a book is due, a time record is kept by filing the book cards or other identity slips behind a date guide in the charging tray. These may be arranged either according to the due date or date of issues, as the case may be. This record is the most essential one since through it the library staff controls and channelises properly the use of books.

Overdues records

Allied to the time record is the Overdues Record. In this record, the information regarding the overdues is kept and the names of the defaulters are entered in it and overdues realised are noted in this record. Though the system of issuing receipts is being used generally, but a new method of conscience Box is being need to avoid the issue of receipts, etc.

Record of issued and reserved books

The books which are issued may be required by other readers. It is essential to know to whom a particular book is issued and when it is due so that a reader may be told to call at the counter on the next approximate date or he may be advised to get the book reserved. In his name. This reservation record is kept alongwith the book records. For the purpose of having a record of issued books, one book card is prepared for each volume and the call number, author, short title, and accession number are provided on the card. The columns for noting down the issue or due dates may be provided if the adopted issue system warrants it. These book cards are filed behind date guides and are arranged either in a classified order or according to the accession number or some other preferred order within the sequence.

Reference department

The Reference Department is the next important service department of a library. The Reference Librarian must maintain the records of the following items so that the record may become accurate basis for evaluating the service rendered to the readers:

1. Nature of the reference books consulted.
2. Nature of enquiries-short or long range.
3. Questions.
4. Answers.
5. Books consulted.
6. Information given.

The information may be recorded so that time may not be wasted for finding out the same information again and again. It is found from experience that the same question is asked very often. The information may be recorded on cards which may be arranged in a order.

Administrative records

A library is a public institution and to run it properly and efficiently a qualified and experienced staff must be employed. This staff must be provided with all facilities such as payment of their salaries within time, sanctioning of leave and promotion according to seniority and merit. For smooth administration, the following records are essential:-

Daily attendance register

This register should be maintained in each library to ensure that every member of the staff attends the library regularly and punctually. In this way, the service at all points is vouchsafed. We can find out from the Daily Attendance Register as to whether a person is present or not. If any person has not marked his presence in this register, it is presumed that he is absent and some alternative arrangement is to be made for providing usual service at the point where the absentee was working.

Duties allocation chart

The office must maintain a 'Duties Allocation Chart". It should be kept up-to-date at all times, so that it can be ascertained at any moment as to where a particular person is working. It would be easier to call him if required. Suppose the library is kept open for twelve hours a day and the staff attends the library in two shifts, It becomes essential to know the names of all the personnel so that. If required any person can be given requisite instructions easily without loss of time.

Causal leave register

A Casual Leave Register should be maintained so that it may be ascertained at any time as to how many days' casual leave has been availed is to his credit still. The register should be in ledger form so that information about a person is found out easily. In other words, one page should be allotted to each person and it should be either arranged serially or alphabetically and it should contain an index. Another kind of record for this purpose can be kept on cards. These may be filed alphabetically.

Privilege and other leave register

Every staff member is allowed certain leave other than casual leave e.g. Privilege leave, medical leave, furlough, study leave, leave without pay etc. A separate ledger type register should be maintained for this purpose since this register is to be maintained for many years. Balance for each person for each kind of leave should be kept up-to-date. This information can also be maintained on cards as suggested in previous paragraph.

Salary register

A permanent Salary Register with usual columns should be maintained so that it can be ascertained at any time as to how much amount was paid to a particular persons as salary. It can be very useful for compiling financial statistics and to provide authentic figures for income-tax and other calculations.

Acquittance rolls register

An Acquittance Rolls Register should be maintained for each office so that a permanent record is kept regarding the disbursement of salaries and other dues to the employees. The receipts should be duly signed and stamped, where necessary.

Gradation list

An accurate Gradation List should be maintained for all employees. It should be according to class, category and post so that it may be ascertained at any time as to who is senior and who is due for promotion. Suppose, a person goes on leave for two months and the next person is to be promoted in his place.

It is essential to ascertain as to who is the right person for purpose, otherwise there would unnecessarily be a lot of ill-will and bad blood amongst the staff members. This list should be kept up-to-date at all times. It must, however, be revised annually without exception so that it may be ascertained as to when a person is due for earning an increment or when a person is due to retire.

Every library should keep all the above-mentioned

records and other minor records up-to-date if an efficient administration is desired.

Maintenance of a records section

In small libraries, each Section keeps its records but in large libraries, a special Records Section becomes essential due to numerous registers and files of various section of the library. Current records are kept in the concerned Section while the completed ones are transferred to the Records Section.

Preparation of the record

Before a record is admitted into the Records Section, it is properly treated. Special labels, identification and location marks indicating the subject, name of the record, year or dates and section are put on each record. Each record, especially looseleaf record, is kept in a appropriate binders, trays or other containers in such a way that their original inner order arrangement is not disturbed.

Arrangement and maintenance of the record

The records may be arranged into two separate sequences i.e., Registers sequences and Files sequence. Within each sequence, the records may be arranged according to their location marks and further in a chronological order if two or more records bear similar location marks.

Issue of the record

A proper record should be kept for each item of the record issued to a Section of the library. Before issuing a particular register/file, a requisition slip and an acknowledgment receipt should be obtained from a responsible/competent person of the concerned Section of the Library. For this purpose, the following Requisition-cum-Issue Card may be maintained:

Record Number	Date of Issue
Section	Signature of the Head of the Receiving Section
Date of requisition	
Date of probable Return	Date of Reminder.
Assistant/Head of the Section	Date of Return
Assistant Librarian.	Record keeper.

At the time of issuing a record, the Record keeper should write down the probable due date of return on the inner side of the covering material i.e. card board in case of a Register, hard file cover in case of a file. The Requisition-cum-Issue Card should be filed in the Issue Tray or Box datewise and sectionwise respectively. If the record is not returned by the probably date, reminder should be issued daily, weekly or monthly, as the case may be. If the record is much overdue, the Record Keeper may get back the concerned record personally or report the facts to the Librarian for necessary orders.

Destruction of the records

It is to be decided as to which records are to be kept permanently and which ones are to be destroyed. In the first category, the following records fall:

1. Accession Registers.
2. Shelf List/Registers.
3. Service Registers.
4. Cadre Registers.
5. Acquittance Rolls register.
6. Application Cards of Members.
7. Cash Security Deposits Registers.
8. Contingent Registers.

9. Monthly and Annual Reports and Statistical Abstracts.

Other records fall in the second category. These may be destroyed after a fixed period, say the years, twenty years or thirty years, according to their value. Specific month of the year should be fixed for the purpose. A senior member of the library staff should be asked to scrutinise the records falling under the second category. Before destroying, specific orders of the Librarian should be obtained for the purpose and all usable parts and mechanisms should be taken off from the registers/files.

9

Managing Library Public Relations

For public relations to be totally successful, the senior library staff have to be persuaded of its value. The senior management team has to believe that public relations can assist in achieving library objectives. It is only when top management appreciate the value of positive public relations that its full impact is felt. It is particularly important for the chief decision-makers in the library organisation to realise that their decisions will affect the image of the library. Thus, in addition to the paid officers valuing PR, it is essential that there is the political will on the part of elected members to make use of public relation methods.

In the past decade, urged on by Skeffington, Maud, and Baines, local authorities in general have increased their public relations activities. Many now have specialised Public Relations Department to advise both elected members and officers. Such departments normally include a press office which issues press releases and generally deals with press matters. In some authorities it is insisted that all press enquiries are handled by the press office and not by the individual departments.

This is part of the corporate dimension of modern local government public relations. Like much of corporate management this has advantages and disadvantages for the public librarian. On the one hand, it means that PR is handled by one or more public relations professionals. On the other, the fact that library publicity has to be channelled through an intermediary can put a further barrier between the library and the audience for which it is intended.

The relationships between the library department and the authority's PR Department are in themselves quite crucial. It is the librarian's responsibility to give the PRO advance warning of events publications, and other matters that he or she wants publicised. Where, as in Lambeth, the Public Relations Department produces a newspaper of its own, this can provide the library service with an extra channel of communication.

A number of librarians, however, have expressed the view that the library's message can sometimes be swamped by the other duties of a local authority's Public Relations Department. Much of British local government PR is concerned with matters such as anti-litter campaigns, or promotions to stop dogs fouling footpaths, or producing posters to persuade people to pay their rates on time. These are of course important subjects, but one wonders if library publicity might not suffer through being associated with them in the mind of the public. In one local authority, such was the feeling against the library being swallowed up in the corporate identify, that the library staff designed, promoted, and used their own departmental logo in preference to that of the parent authority. There is the further point as to whether public relations staff, more used to designing campaigns of the 'stop dogs fouling footpath' variety, are the best-equipped people to promote the rather different library message.

Library PR departments

In the United States, many libraries have their own Public relations Departments, some employing specialist journalists, artists, photographers and broadcasters. In a paper prepared for the 1978 ALA pre-conference on library public relations, Kathleen Rummel suggested that a library with 50 to 100 full-time equivalent (FTE) staff should have 2 FTE persons assigned to PR, while in a library with 100 FTE staff and above there should be 'a base of 2 FTE persons assigned to PR with one additional staff person for every 100 staff.

In the British public library context, separate Public Relations Departments simply do not exist. Some authorities, such as Leicestershire, have posts designated for a PR librarian, while other employ publications officers (e.g. Sheffield) and graphic designers (e.g., Shropshire County). With the exception of the graphic designers, most of these posts have been filled by professional librarians rather than by people professionally qualified in public relations.

There are some advantages in employing professional PR personnel. In general, the press and broadcasting organisations prefer dealing with fellow journalists. The media organisations also tend to feel that a professional public relations person will prepare and present materials in the right form for them to use. It is also true that a PR professional is, initially at least, likely to have more contracts than a librarian entering the work for the first time.

Both professional librarians and professional public relations people should have communication skills, and there is no doubt that the right kind of librarian can do a very effective PR job. In additions, library public relations does require a person who can understand the library and its functions. Whoever undertakes library PR must be the type who can take the initiative. He or she must also possess sound judgment and really believe in the importance of the library client. Good public relations is not just a matter of informing people about the library and its services, it is also very much about listening to people, to their ideas, enquiries, and complaints.

Volunteers

Some public relations activities lend themselves to the employment of volunteer labour. For example, some libraries use trained volunteers as tour guides. Quite reasonably, trade union members object to volunteers doing a job that should be carried out by paid members of staff. For the sake of good staff' management relationships, consultations with appropriate union representatives should always take place before unpaid help is employed.

Training

It is the task of management to ensure that all staff are aware of the importance of public relations. There may be resistance on the part of some librarians who think that public relations is merely a series of circus acts below their professional dignity. The function of positive public relations should be explained to them; in particular it is necessary to emphasise the importance of human relations.

The earlier this is done the better. Every induction programme for new staff should include a section on dealing with people. A course designed for a new assistant might include all or some of the following:

1. An explanation of the library's policy on everyday matters, such as smoking, wheelchairs, rowdyism, dogs, etc.

2. A session on how to deal with complaints and when to refer them to more senior members of staff.
3. The use of the telephone.
4. Local bylaws.
5. Interpretation of rules and regulations.

Above all, such a course should stress the importance of high standards of service and behavior.

In addition to induction course, some libraries include public relations in their general training programmes. Training can play a part in changing staff attitudes to PR. However, this is a long-term process and it would be foolish to suggest that entrenched attitudes can be changed by just one course. As convenor of the Sheffield Libraries Coordinating Committee's Working Party on the Training and Education, the writer was involved in the presentation of a course on library public relations. The course itself was very successful, but a number of participants made the point that the people who would have most benefited from it did not attend. This is perhaps an example of selective exposure mechanisms at work within our own field! In recent years Buckinghamshire and Shropshire Country Libraries have both devoted their annual training courses to public relations, making use of their own staff and outside speakers. In general, however, public relations has not featured in enough internal or external training courses.

The staff manual should also include a section on public relations. Indeed, the philosophy of PR should permeate all sections of the manual, especially those dealing with rules and regulations; management should decide just how many rules and regulations are really necessary. Restrictive regulations should be kept to a minimum and where rules do exist, staff should be encouraged to interpret them liberally. Very often junior staff can appear unnecessarily bureaucratic to the client, not because it is in their nature but because they do not have the confidence to bend the rules. It is up to senior management to encourage staff to give people priority over petty procedures. Too many public services in Britain seem to be organised to catch the 1 per cent who abuse them, rather than to help the 99 per cent who want to use them.

Libraries need not, and should not, be organised in this ay. It is up to senior staff to set the right style.

One is both encouraged and discouraged by the views of chief librarians on this subject. The diversity of approach is well illustrated by the discussion that took place at a recent meeting of chief librarians. At one extreme there were those who were advocating a new and complicated procedure for registering out-of-authority readers, while on the other there were those who, quite rightly, wanted to make joining any library service as simple as possible, It is worth emphasising that this was a meeting at which the librarians were free from direct political constraints and could express their own views, In so doing, they demonstrated their own attitudes towards the public they serve-attitudes which they are also, no doubt, communicating directly and indirectly to their staff.

No doubt, those who advocated stricter control of membership did so on the basis that they would be saving public money. This in itself is arguable, but what is more significant is the costs of such a policy, to individual library systems and to librarianship as a whole, in terms of public relations. For those members of the public faced with such a petty restriction, the library becomes just another bureaucratic organisation placing barriers between the client and the service he or she requires. The person who is already suspicious or frightened of local authorities may not try to join again.

This is not to say that costs are not important: on one would argue that in today's economic climate. Library management needs to be aware of the costs of public relations, but equally it needs to be aware of the costs of not allocating resources to public relations-costs such as lack of public interest or decreased public an political support for the library service.

Public relations rarely appears as a separate budget item in a British public library's estimates. In fact, such a heading is relatively rare in the United States where there is a tendency to call it something else. Also in the US many libraries include programming (talks, film, shows, concerts, etc.) under the same heading a public relations. This makes and assessment of the size of the 'pure' PR budget difficult. Rummel suggests that 'a rule of thumb is that 10-15% of your budget should be applied to public relations, community relations, and programming.

When calculating the costs of public relations, it is important to include all the costs involved. For example, the costs of issuing a press release will includes some or all of the following:

1 The cost of posting X number of copies.

2 A percentage of the cost of the office equipment used to prepare and reproduce the release.

3 The cost of stationery used.

4 The costs of any photographs included with the release.

5. Staff costs (time spent creating and writing the release, time spent typing the release, time spent duplicating, etc.).

With PR as with any aspect of management, it is vital to know how and why money has been spent.

Planning

Expenditure on public relations has to be carefully planned. Indeed, planning and preparation can make or break a library's public relations activities. PR should be planned to achieve clearly defined objectives. The planning process needs to include a consideration of the human and other resources available to help attain these objectives, an estimate of the financial resources required, and an indication of target dates for achieving objectives. Priorities will, of course, have to be established within any given timetable.

Once overall objectives and priorities have been ascertained and consideration given to the resources needed, the library public relations person is in a position to consider specific matters of detail. As part of this process it is necessary to look at the library service through the eyes of the library's various publics. Clients, staff, non-users, legislators, and suppliers will all have different perceptions of the library and its services. For each of these groups the library will have, in balance-sheet terms, PR assets and PR liabilities. Senior library management should seek to identify these assets and liabilities as an integral part of their public relations planning.

In a typical public library, assets light include helpful assistants an accessible location, a reliable reference service, and so on. Liabilities could include belligerent staff, erratic overdue procedure, negative notices, and the like. One of the functions of library PR is to reduce such liabilities to a minimum. By paying close attention to all aspects of the service, it is possible to draw up a public relations balance sheet listing those things which help and those which hinder the library's image.

On the basis of such preparation, one can begin to produce a practical programme of activities tailored to the library's needs and resources. It will be necessary to plan some things well in advance, but a PR programme also needs to be flexible, so that the library service can quickly respond to new events and demands.

As a vital part of a library's internal public relations it is essential to involve staff in the public relations planning process. As stated earlier, there may be staff who are suspicious of the value of the whole idea and it is especially necessary to secure their cooperation and support. There is no easy way of doing this but certainly it will be much difficult if plans are announced to them without any warning.

10

PUBLIC LIBRARY TRAINING

Within labour intensive organisations such as public libraries the establishment budget accounts for the principal part of the annual expenditure. It is imperative, therefore, that this costly resource is utilised by managers and supervisors alike, with as much skill and expertise as possible. Library authorities can spend as much as 60-70 per cent of their total annual budget on staffing, a significant amount when one considers that as little as 15-20 per cent is spent on the 'lifeblood of the service'-books. Whilst these figures are only generalisations and will vary slightly from authority to authority the proportions can make startling reading.

Personnel management is a 'root and branch' consideration, not to be left to a few interested 'management types' at the top of the tree. Everyone, from first line supervisors to the chief librarian, must play a part in ensuring that there is efficient use of their subordinates, and one of the corner-stones of this efficient use is training.

Looking back over the last few years public libraries have been affected by many changes, some from within the profession, some from outside. These changes have inevitably had a bearing on the services of the public libraries and indeed, at times, their ability to offer a 'comprehensive and efficient service' as required by the 1964 Public Libraries and Museums Act. In addition many of these changes have affected staffing resources, and some of these are mentioned below.

Since the reorganisation of local government in 1974 Public Library Authorities are much larger organisations, which have tried, in many cases, to offer a broader base of service than hitherto. One of the consequences has been the development of more specialised functions and roles for library staff at all levels, and there has been a shift in emphasis in what libraries traditionally provide. For instance, the growth of Team Librarianship had meant a complete reappraisal of functions and skills and such massive changes create both opportunities and problems in the management and training of staff.

There are many examples of training programmes formulated by public library authorities which are designed to cover a whole spectrum of activities. One can find specimens of programmes designed to cover everything an inner-city service, and some of these will be considered later.

One of the depressing influences affecting public libraries (and in fact many service industries) over the last few years has been the economic climate pertaining in the United Kingdom. After a relatively expansionist period during the late 1960s and early 1970s public libraries, generally, have been made to tighten their belts since the mid-seventies and the cold realities of the eighties have meant that phrases such as 'rate capping', 'procurement cuts' are common parlance in library circles. In the need to economise one of the major targets has been staffing, often with a view to protecting the book fund, but this has come doubly hard at a time when there has been increasing demand on services and a push from within the profession to diversify and widen the scope of provision to the users. It has become, therefore, increasingly important to maximise the potential of existing staff and in this instance training has a substantial role to play. The Library Association Working Party on Training emphasised this point in its report:

> Training is not a luxury, and optional extra which can be indulged in only in good times when finance is available and staff are plentiful. In fact, the reverse is true; when time are hard and all resources have to be fully and efficiently used, the need for training is greater than ever. To sacrifice training to short term economies is a failure of vision.

A more positive factor influencing training has been the realisation by many authorities that it should be tackled on a systematic basis, and one way of ensuring this has been to appoint specialist officers to organise and generate activity in this field. In some cases this has been a full-time training officer, in other cases a personnel function is involved. Less preferably, and more commonly, officers who already carry other responsibilities are nominated to act as the training specialist, apparently in their spare time! Larger authorities such as Manchester, Birmingham and some countries have had specialist personnel sections, including training officers, within the Libraries Department for many years but the last decade has seen a growth in the employment of library training officers both in countries and Metropolitan District either based entirely in the department or operating from a central personnel unit.

The factors mentioned above have had a very mixed influence on staff resources in public libraries. In recent years many unpalatable decisions regarding library personnel have had to be taken, but the need to train is nevertheless paramount. Without training we are perhaps jeopardising our relationship with and services to the public who still regard libraries as one of the more acceptable faces of local government. The librarian must employ all the abilities he or she has as manager in order to maintain existing services as well as introduce new ones, and one of the most effective strategies he or she can use is a well organised and effective training programme. Public libraries have a wealth of resources on which they can draw, both external and internal, to achieve good training practices. These include their own staff, with specialist knowledge and skills, who can be used on internal programmes and courses and local authorities' personnel departments, which can help with general principles and guidance as well as participating in training. Polytechnics, colleges and library schools may be willing to offer their services either in direct nearby library authorities could possibly share the cost of training as well as help organise programmes on a co-operative basis. The Library Association and other similar bodies regularly organise courses and organisations allied to local government, such as the local Government Training Board, will assist in the setting up of programmes in addition to giving advice on training.

Given the necessary commitment there is no reason why good training practices should not be achieved. A half-hearted 'short in the dark' is not to be recommended, though unfortunately this happens all too often. A systematic more positive examples of public library training programmes are described.

This is one area of training which is essential and for lack of which there can be no excuse! If systematic training is being organised then this is an obvious starting point. Many textbooks, guidance manuals and accounts of existing practices are readily available to assist the would-be-trainer.

One basic text, which given examples, is the Library Association's Sub-Committee on Training Guidelines for Training in Libraries-Systematic Induction, written by P. Robertson. This deals with areas such as the different categories of employees benefiting from induction, the special needs of schools leaves, the training of those responsible for induction, checklists and the use of other resources.

Many public library authorities have well-developed induction programmes, for example Bolton, Cambridgeshire, Hampshire, Sheffield, Tameside an Trafford. Trafford's programme includes an induction package in the form of a folder which is handed to new starters on their first morning at work. The folder contains the appropriate job description, a statement of particulars relating to their conditions of service a number of 'in-house' forms to be completed by the employee and two copies of an induction checklist. There is also an introductory booklet which outlines the work of the library service, describes the major conditions of services, gives a general guide to the locality, including bus and rail routes, and a further reading list which may help the new recruit during the first few weeks of employment. This information pack is backed up by a welcome from a senior member of staff, guided induction training by the appropriate supervisor as well as a four-day induction course which usually occurs within the first six months of employment.

Cambridgeshire and Hampshire both have comprehensive induction checklists and detailed instructions relevant to particular posts, whilst Derbyshire provides a checklist for induction of pre-licentiates. Although checklists are now regarded as a traditional form of induction training it is fundamentally important that they are properly understood and used by the supervisor concerned.

Without skilful manipulation the checklist can become so much waste paper to be consigned to someone's personal file, never to re-appear, and, crucially, never to have been of any use in the formative period of someone's employment. The introduction of such a checklist is a beginning but its utilisation by trained supervisors is critical, and to ensure that the qualitative as well as the quantitative aspect of the checklist is secured it is essential that supervisors themselves are fully trained in their use. Some authorities have accompanying evaluation of their induction programme so that at the end of a given time, usually between three and six months, a report on the progress of the new recruit is complied and examined. Trafford Libraries have such a system, a detailed report on the employee's ability, character and potential being sent to the personnel officer by the supervisor. Any remedial action, including re-training, can then be subsequently taken, as necessary.

Other methods and techniques can be used in induction, depending on circumstances. Many country library authorities which are geographically diverse face particular difficulties in ensuring systematic and uniform training and centralised induction, but even some of the most rural have evolved excellent programmes. Cornwall Country Libraries employ a modular approach to their training and this is described in detail in their Staff Training Manual.

Different modules are available to suit the particular level of members of staff being inducted, thus ensuring a uniform approach under difficult geographic circumstances. Bolton employs a modular approach to induction courses for library assistants through l half- and one-day course. Other formal aspects of their induction training include a detailed checklist and an interview with a senior member of staff at the end of the first twelve-month period. Derbyshire organises regular headquarters familiarization courses both for new recruits and established members of staff. These course, of three days duration, enable staff to have an opportunity to hear about the work done by the headquarters of a large country library system.

Hampshire Country Library holds similar course for both professionals and assistants which are carried out at the library headquarters, whilst Birmingham Libraries have a five day induction course for librarians and assistants held at three separate venues throughout the week. An important element of this course is public relations training and this is particularly emphasised by the City Librarian in his introduction to the course programme. This area of what one can term attitude training should be uppermost in the trainer's mind during induction. It is relatively straightforward to teach and explain man routines and systems, but not always so easy to inculcate the correct attitudes expected of the staff. However, one can expect problems at a later stage from the new recruit and from their colleagues and supervisors if this aspect is neglected.

There is no obvious single method of induction training relevant in every situation, and it is reassuring to see the determined and varied efforts made by public libraries in tackling this important area of training. For those about to embark upon systematic induction programmes I would strongly recommend the Library Associations's publications mentioned previously as a suitable starting point.

Job training and instruction

Job training, sometimes known as 'sitting next to Nellie', is practised universally in all organisations either consciously or unconsciously. However, as Ronald Edwards has said:

> There tends to be an easy assumption that satisfactory job training exists because every one who remains in post in a library must of necessity have learnt his job to at least minimum standards.

This common assumption must, as Edwards implies, be challenged by all trainers. Although the instruction of staff takes many forms, for example the simple command or the planned learning programme, it fails to be effective unless the training is given at the optimum time by the most appropriate person.

Unfortunately, there is often a tendency on the part of librarians to equate training with short courses carried out away from the work area, but in fact a great deal of the learning process takes place on-site either through direct instruction or through serendipity, the sink or swim approach!

It is important that each facet of the job is taught effectively to the trainee, and the key element involved here is the quality of the trainer. Wirral Library Service hold a two-day, in-house course which covers the main areas associated with the organisation and execution of library training. The emphasis is on a participative approach by course members, and involves role-play, group discussions and case studies designed to simulate live situations in the work place.

Traffored Library Service's four-day supervisory course for junior professionals includes one day devoted entirely to training, with the emphasis on job training and instruction. There is a mixture of lectures outlining in a practical way the various elements of systematic training, and this is followed by a participative session where each course member plans and carries out a simple instructional programme using other members as the 'trainee', Sheffield City Libraries have also identified job training and development as an important area. They have held seminars for large numbers of staff on the principles of on-the-job development training, and are planning courses on counselling and coaching skills for librarians and supervisors. Sheffield has also introduced a self-learning scheme for the Youth Training Scheme trainees within the library service. Instead of the traditional guided tour of the library a Central Library Trail is used in which the trainees, in pairs, explore various departments following guidance notes and instructions provided to them at the outset. There are questions to be answered along the way, and if all else fails they are instructed to ask the staff! In all the five trails covering the departments of the central Library. This is an interesting methods of guided self-discovery which should help in the familiarisation process, and replaces what may be a rather uninteresting piece of conventional instruction form a trainer.

One method more widely employed by public libraries, particularly in the training of library assistants, is that of job rotation. It naturally benefits the trainee to become familiar with all aspects of the library's work in which he or she may have to become involved in the future, and at the same time alleviates the problems of boredom and disinterest. Careful consideration must be given, however, to the regularity of the rotation to ensure that adequate time is allowed for staff to assimilate the necessary skills associated with a new work situation. Clear verbal and written instruction must of course be given at each stage.

Staff training manuals can either be a help of a liability in job training, depending largely on their accuracy, up-to-training in mind, using a lucid, step-by-step approach to each facet. They should be used to confirm rather than inform once initial job training is complete.

Leicestershire Libraries and Information Service developed their job training programme through the use of packages to cover certain areas of work, including the 'effective use of team time', 'issue and counter routines' and 'basic enquiry work'. This latter package is still used and comprises notes and programmed instructions on the basics of handling requests and dealing with enquiries in the library, along with examples of the necessary stationery. This type of training can be used for small groups of trainees, or on a one-to-one basis, and enables a uniform and consistent approach to be achieved. It is surprising that this method has not been adopted on a wider scale, particularly where many of the clerical and administrative routines lend themselves to a programmed learning approach.

Job training, therefore, requires a well planned and systematic approach from the trainer. The key element is the quality of 'Nellie' and therefore training the trainer must be the first priority.

Off-the job training

Off-the-job training is often dealt with in summary

fashion by the 'we'll send them on a course' attitude, and it is easy to be led into the subtle trap of using courses, both internal and external as a substitute for properly organised job training. The aim should be a blend of the two, each being used at the appropriate time in a person's training and development

Handled skillfully, of course, off-the-job training constitutes a much needed ingredient of staff development both for present post held as well as preparation for a future role the trainee may have in the organisation.

As the term implies, off-the-job training takes place away from the work site, and can take many diverse forms- short term secondments to other departments or sections of the service, for example, or educational/training courses such as the City and Guilds Library Assistants' Certificate or the BEC/ COTEC Certificates which include modules on library studies. Internal and external courses, formal and informal group discussions and seminars are also an integral part of off-the-job training.

Trainers often have an ambivalent attitude to the relative merits of external and internal courses. Internal course, if well prepared and carried out can be a much more cost effective methods of training because they can maximise the use of existing resources within the organisation. It is often possible to hide any necessary expenditure and the training itself may be more valid because it can be tailored directly to the needs of the participants. External courses have to be the paid for in hard cash which necessarily limits the number of staff able to attend, particularly if there are high add-on costs such as subsistence of external courses is often difficult for the Training Officer and the exact level and content of the course sometimes impossible to ascertain.

On the other hand external courses often fulfil a specific training need for a small number or even individual members of staff which could not effectively be dealt with internally. Similarly courses organised in-house may have the disadvantage of seeming amateurish, of being too close to home, resulting in interruptions, hit-and-miss attendance through staffing difficulties, or poor presentations by speakers who themselves have not been properly briefed. The Library Association's Working Party on Training gives a basic guide to assessing internal and external courses.

Turning now to externally-based training, and the use made of it by public libraries, there has undoubtedly been a strong tradition amongst organisations in the field of librarianship to offer short duration courses, both nationally and regionally. The Library Association and its groups, notably the Association of Assistant librarians and the Youth Libraries Group, organise many courses across a wide curriculum, a list of which is published in the Record. Other bodies such as ASLIB individual colleges of librarianship and even individual library authorities offer short duration courses on a national and regional basis. Some of these organisations also offer courses covering a particular aspect of study. This has been examples in recent years by courses provided by the College of Librarianship Wales and the North West Division of the Association of Assistant Librarians. In the case of CLW the expertise is drawn directly from the college's own resources, thus providing a relatively inexpensive method of training a number of staff. The AAL courses can be taken to a particular authority and be geared specifically to the needs and requirements of their particular staff. General subjects such as supervisory and personnel management are areas that perhaps best lend themselves to this type of arrangement. There may not be a pool of expertise within the individual authority or there may be other domestic difficulties preventing the organisation of internal courses, and, therefore, this type of training can alleviate these problems.

Individual library authorities have, within the last few years offered courses in particular subjects to other public libraries. Two notable examples of this are the London Borough of Sutton, which has arranged one-day courses on Merchandising within the Library, and Northamptonshire Country Library's course on Local History Publications. Again this is an excellent method of using a skill by a particular authority, sharing their expertise with other libraries which may not have the necessary resources to set up an internal course.

It has been said earlier that job training activities form a basic equipment within an organisation, but any public library with a commitment to training will appreciate that there are certain types of training which require staff to be away from the distractions and hurly-burly of their jobs. Public libraries such as Cornwall, Sheffield and Renfrew all have well developed in-house programmes. Cornwall's Staff Training Manual lists training and development courses for all levels of staff from Assistant Country Librarian to Library Assistant and this encompasses a whole range of modules for each category of staff. Sheffield City Libraries organise internal programmes in a variety of topics. Their one-day customer relations courses use exercises, questionnaires and role-plays as well as extensive audio-visual material. This type of course can be invaluable not only for new recruits but for the more experienced member of staff. Reference was made under Induction' to the need for attitude training, not only for the new starter but also for others who have worked in the organisation for some time who may not always have picked up the right habits when it comes to dealing with people. Emphasis can easily be placed on the nuts and bolts of clerical and administrative training whilst attitude and interpersonal skills take a back seat, either because they are thought too difficult to teach or merely because of an assumption that everyone knows how to deal with the public anyway.

One current area of debate is the development aspect of training and in view of some of the obstacles previously mentioned (financial constraints, etc.) this is becoming a matter of concern. Brief mention has already been made of some of the lengthier training/educational courses available for library staff and this is obviously a very fruitful methods of ensuring their development, both as individuals and as members of the workforce. Whilst it can be argued that some courses are primarily educational, one cannot discount their effectiveness in enhancing knowledge, skills and attitudes.

Some public libraries regard the BBC/SCOTEC and City and Guilds Certificate as a prerequisite for promotion and offer secondment to one or more staff annually. Larger systems, such as Lancashire Country Libraries, are very generous in enabling a number of assistants to attend. The courses are usually organised by Further Education and Technical Colleges, and support by public libraries has been quite encouraging.

The City and Guilds Certificate, the shorter of the courses, is of one year's duration and is essentially a practical introduction to libraries and library skills. Students usually attend for half day per week with an examination at the end of the course. It is a fairly gentle introduction to the work of the library for staff wishing to know more about the background to their job. The course covers areas such as the organisation of libraries, arrangements of stocks and use of the catalogue, loan and circulation procedures and office practice in libraries.

The BEC/SCOTEC courses, leading to the National Diploma, are much broader based and more intensive courses. Students are expected to attend for a full day per week for two years. Subjects other than library studies are an integral part of the course and these include accountancy, economic, statistics and the role of the organisation in the environment. The library studies module forms approximately one quarter of the course.

Although one might be tempted to argue that this constitutes too small a percentage of the whole, the benefits accruing to the individual may outweigh the disadvantages. The broader base of subjects covered helps to widen horizons and give better understanding on other facets of local government. Some authorities have found that staff seconded who more aware of their role within the organisation but are capable of assuming greater responsibilities. It is, in addition, a potential stepping stone to higher academic achievement either at university, college or library school.

A relatively new innovation in Scotland has been the introduction of a correspondence course leading to the Scottish Certificate in library and information science. The course lasts for two years and is organised by the Telford college of Further Education in Edinburgh. Students are sent forty-four student units, one every two weeks, and there is a residential week each session at the college. Each student has a personal tutor at the college who keeps in touch and assessment is by regular assignments and college examinations in the residential weeks. He college is also adapting the study units to a produce a one year's course leading to the city and Guilds Certificate for library assistants, will have to spend their own time studying for such a qualification although one hopes that there will be some financial acknowledgment and reward by the employer both during and at the end of the course.

For professional staff there are courses, usually leading to a qualification, such as the BA conversion, and the part-time post graduate courses in librarianship, as well as various management based programmes such as the Diploma in Management Studies and MA Librarianship, the latter being offered by a number of library schools. Recently, all these courses have become popular and public libraries have supported their staff on them.

It is, however, the responsibility of the training officer and/or the supervisor to assess and monitor the progress of the member of staff attending such a course. Regular counselling and discussion sessions should be organised to ensure that the person concerned is able to cope with the work and the commitment involved. These sessions also enable a check to be kept on the organisation and content of the course to see whether or not the objectives are being achieved. Sending staff on these lengthy courses is expensive and the trainer must make sure it is not being wasted.

Developmental training within the organisation is also an areas which public libraries have recognised as being essential. There is, of course, no clearly defined line between this type of training and that relating and that relating to a person's specific job, as one tends to evolve from the other. Many of the external professional courses mentioned earlier may form an integral part of a person's development and it may often be the only method that some public libraries use to help staff in this way. Some authorities, however, have taken a more positive approach, realising that there is a need to develop their staff in a more planned and structured way. Certainly few library systems can claim similar training programmes established by examples within the private sector where their managers are pushed through development 'hoops' for most of their working lives, but there are examples where determined efforts have been made. Liverpool City Libraries in conjunction with the department of Management at the Liverpool Polytechnic have organised development courses for their senior staff, lasting five days. A variety of topics include resource allocation, identification of problems in managing public libraries and an appreciation of performance counselling using a problem-centered approach. The first of these was reported as being highly successful and the course will be repeated as often as necessary.

Derbyshire Country Libraries development training is carried out either in-house through courses specifically for library staff or through the Manpower Services Division of the Country Council who offer an annual programme of courses, including management development activities. Some of the topics covered within this area are management of human behaviour, a middle management programme and post professional training. There is a similar arrangement in Tame-side where the central Personnel department offer a variety of general courses aimed at officers within the whole organisation.

Wirral Library Service has also recognised a need for developmental training both through internal and external programmes. In responses to new initiative within the service, such as the introduction of new technology, courses are organised for both professional staff and assistants. Trafford Library Service has recently been looking at this area following discussions by the Authority with the Local Government Training Board. A working party has been established to examine in more detail what can be achieved given the limited resources and other problems such as in-built resistance by some staff to participate in any formally organised scheme! Their considerations have been, up to now, related to management rather than professional development, which may result in a widening of roles for managers and even inter-departmental secondments in the future.

Development training, therefore, is of immense importance in public libraries, particularly at a time when a variety of skills and expertise is expected of staff at all levels, combined with an increasingly demanding public and scarcity of resources. As with other training, however, it must be carefully managed. It is a failure by the organisation and manager if this type of training is not given due recognition for there are everyday examples where staff can and need to be prepared for more difficult and demanding tasks, maybe within the scope of their present job as well for roles they may assume in the future, demanding higher degrees of knowledge and skills. Professional staff in particular are expected to carry our jobs which they may never have considered within the scope of a librarian when they first entered the profession and whilst it can be argued that times change and staff must be adaptable, the onus is one the organisation to ensure they are encouraged and helped through well planned developmental training, either on or off the job.

A relatively recent introduction in training has been co-operative ventures between public libraries as well as university and college libraries. There are obvious advantages and benefits in that there is a sharing of expertise, costs, accommodation as well as interaction between staff with varying experience and attitudes. Two examples of such co-operation are in the North East of England and in South Yorkshire where local Training Officer groups have been established to discuss training matters within libraries, and in addition, take a positive approach by organising programmes for staff of the various libraries within the area. The North East group was established in 1980 and, with the support and encouragement of the Local Government Training Board, has provided courses on interpersonal and communication skills and on coaching and counselling staff. An account of their activities in the first two years has been written by Ralph Major who describes the tangible results of the co-operative venture. As well as the two courses mentioned above, these include a compilation of training resources, and co-operation between libraries in enabling staff to attend each other's internal courses. One course arranged by the group on computerisation was a very co-operative affair involving not only public libraries but also the Department of Librarianship at Newcastle Polytechnic and members of the book trade. The LGTB, too, have assisted on their coaching and counselling skills course.

In Sheffield there is a Libraries Co-ordinating Committee involving the city library, university and colleges and within this group is a working party on the education and training of library staff which, as with the North East co-operative venture, organises courses for staff of the various libraries. The local training officer group (LTOG) in South Yorkshire libraries, organises courses and exchange of experience seminars as well as an annual debate on a current topic of interest within the profession to which all library staff in the area are invited.

These schemes are excellent examples of how training can be organised on a co-operative basis. Where one or more libraries may not have the time, financial resources or expertise to arrange off-the -job training a co-operative venture could certainly help, although it would be wise to seek advice before attempting to set one up. It has to be a truly co-operative exercise with everyone playing a part rather than a couple of willing workhorse doing all the arranging and keeping the group together. Inevitably in these circumstances co-operative will not last long! The fourth of the Library Association's Guidelines on training, written by Alan MacDougall, deals with this very subject and gives sound practical advice on setting one up.

Off-the-job training provides a splendid opportunity to use a variety of techniques to help and stimulate the trainee which often cannot be used, or would simply be inappropriate within a job-training programme. Many of the courses mentioned above use case studies, role plays, simulation and in-tray exercises to help in learning. Provided that these techniques are used appropriately within the programme they can often make telling points which the trainee will remember. However, there is often an understandable reluctance on the part of staff to participate in an exercise in which they may be made to look foolish in front of their peer group and it is, therefore, the responsibility of the trainer to make certain that all instructions are clearly understood and that staff are not unnecessarily embarrassed by any such device.

There is also, an excellent range of films, video and tape/slide presentations which can contribute much to a particular training situation and these can either be made in-house, by Video Arts. Certain areas of training lend themselves particularly to the use of A/V materials, for example interpersonal skills and supervisory work. Perhaps Health & Safety at Work is the obvious example where films etc., can form the focal point of the training. A clear and concise tape/slide presentation made by Cheshire Libraries and Museums Service some years ago is a good example of libraries using this material. It is highly relevant in that it describes problems specifically associate with health and safety in the library and can be used either with small or large groups or even as part of the induction of a new member of staff. The other benefit is that it is portable and can be shown any where, thus saving time on having to organise a programme at one central point.

Wirral Library Service in-operation with the college of Librarianship Wales has recently produced a tape/slide package on working with the public, which forms the basis of on-going training in branch libraries. This is the first in a series to be produced by CLW, aimed at library assistants, and may be purchases by other library authorities or individuals.

Salford and Bolton Libraries have each produced in-house videos. Bolton's film entitled All in a day's work deals with public relations, and Salford's on story telling to children. Both authorities use them in the context of training programmes for professional staff and assistants.

Looking generally at the activity of training in public libraries there have been major efforts made in certain areas during the last few years. Induction training has been recognised as a crucial aspect of the librarian's and supervisor's work and by now the majority of systems at least appear to make use of the checklist. Other training seems to be a more hit-and-miss affair with some authorities having a co-ordinated systematic approach whilst other claim that time and money is not available, and therefore, formalised training must suffer.

Role of the training officer

Obviously one of the key figures concerned with public library training is the designated training officer. Large public library systems such as Birmingham and Manchester have employed specialist training staff for some years, and whilst many authorities still do not have such a full-time post within the libraries department there has been a growing recognition of the need for an officer at an executive level to control training and there are examples, even in the smaller metropolitan districts, of such officers. Admittedly, there are many examples where their time is not exclusively given over to training, and there are examples, even in the smaller metropolitan districts, of such officers. There are many examples where their time is not exclusively given over to training, and their posts may encompass other managerial and operational duties.

There have been numerous reports in recent years which recommend the appointment of a designated training officer.

Foremost of these is the Library Association Education Committee Working Party on post-qualification training, published in 1974. Research undertaken by LAMSAC for the Department of Education and Science, which subsequently formed the report 'Staffing of Public Libraries', also supports this by recommending one training officer for every 200 non-manual staff, but admits that so much depends upon the training policies of the overall authority.

The duties of the training officer are to establish a training policy for the library service in conjunction with his/her fellow management officers, and then to implement the policy-by co-ordinating and generating appropriate training activities. He or she generally 'oils the wheels' of training rather than engaging in its direct policy on a day-to-day basis. The role is to establish priorities, assess needs in co-operation with line managers and supervisors, organise the most appropriate form of training, liaise with other personnel inside and outside the organisation and carry out the administrative duties of training officer will also attempt to measure the effectiveness of training using evaluation and validation techniques, although to be candid, this is a difficult area which appears not to have been developed to any depth in the public library field. An equally important role for this officer is to ensure that line managers and supervisors are themselves trained in the techniques of training, and some public libraries have recognised this as a significant prerequisite to sound training practice by organising programmes for appropriate officers.

One particular category of staff which should be highlighted in relation to public library training is the licentiate and pre-licentiate. Libraries have always recognised the problem of the newly qualified member of staff, fresh from library schools with little or no practical experience, but expected to assume responsibilities and carry out duties with which they are not always familiar, and more importantly, in which they have received no training. Unfortunately, not everyone has come to grips with the problem and this was recognised by the Working Party on the Future of Professional Qualifications which endeavoured in its report and recommendation to tighten up the Library Association's requirements for a much fuller and wider ranging training programmes for post-qualification staff. This was endorsed by the Library Association Council and has been in operation sine 1982. Public libraries, by and large, have responded to this requirement in a positive way. For each pre-licentiate recruited a programme must be submitted to the Library Association for formal vetting and approval. This system is intended to ensure that the newly qualified member of staff will receive a sound practical training programme in their duties as well as background information on the work of the library and any other area necessary to equip them for a professional job in the future. This also applies, incidentally, to people appointed to temporary posts, such as schemes funded by the Manpower Services commission, and libraries must recognise their responsibility to offer appropriate training in the same way as with full-time, permanent appointments, whether or not the member of staff concerned is likely to finish the pre-licentiate year with that particular scheme.

Newcastle City Libraries have an excellent programme which has been completed by five pre-licentiates to date, and which has, naturally, been further developed in the light of experience since its inception. The aims and objectives of pre-licentiateship are outlined in the written programme, including the responsibilities of the supervising librarian and the requirements of the Library Association in acceptance of the candidate for licentiateship. The important element of induction is included, along with the general framework and core areas recommended by the Library Association. The component parts of these areas are professional practices (e.g. book selection, stock maintenance, readers' advisory and enquiry work), technical skills (e.g. book acquisition, use of specialised bibliographical tools and equipment) and interpersonal skills, including basic supervisory, management and training responsibilities

The programme itself is arranged on a modular basis in order to give a certain degree of flexibility, each module varying in length according to the function and scope of the section or department involved. The co-ordination of the overall programme is done by the City Librarian, and in terms of the Library Association's requirements he is the supervising librarian. The pre-licentiates meet the City Librarian on a monthly basis for discussion and progress reviews, and arrangements are also made for their visits, projects and logbook of training and experience.

Trafford Library Service has a full programme for pre-licentiates. This comprises various elements including on-the-job training, an important aspect because the pre-licentiate is appointed to a specific post and is, therefore, not extra to the establishment. Off-the-job training constitutes secondments and attachments to various sections and libraries lasting from three days to two weeks, and visits to other library systems. The pre-licentiate also completes a detailed logbook which is

examined prior to the monthly meeting with one of the Assistant Borough Librarians and carries out a project which is of a practical nature and, where possible, contributes to the work of the Department. A final lengthy interview with the Borough Librarian and other appropriate senior staff to discuss the training year in general, and the project in particular, rounds off the programme. The licentiate-to-be is given opportunities to continue his/her professional development through attendance at course, meetings and working parties, and is encouraged to join in professional activities of the Association.

A further area of training in which public libraries have been strongly involved is that of library schools field work. Many authorities have recognised that it is important for librarians to assist in the training of the newest 'recruits' to the profession and whilst, as in other training areas, there are good and had examples of fieldwork training, in general public libraries expend a lot of time and effort in ensuring the student is given a sound programme during the limited time they are seconded to libraries. It is easy for experienced staff to criticize the quality of post library schools applicants for jobs, but unfortunately, not so easy to give a commitment to their training in the formative' period within the profession, bearing in mind particularly the nature of library education vis-a-vis practical experience. Many public libraries organise well balanced fieldwork placements which cover a mixture of practical experience through working in one or more sections or departments of the library with opportunities to see and hear about the majority of the library's service through visits and discussions with appropriate departmental staff.

Community librarianship

One particular area of training to which public libraries have given recognition during the last few years has been in response to a change in emphasis of the nature of library services and a growing awareness of the need to become more attuned to the requirements of their communities. Community librarianship, the commonly used term for this change, can involve the preparation of community profiles, the establishment of a community information service as well as the traditional advice and research involved in reference librarianship. There are obvious implications here for the education, training and recruitment of staff. This type of librarianship requires an approach and image which many be far removed from the traditional one, and training is one of the key factors in this brave new world.

Community librarianship, particularly inner city provision can be an extremely sensitive area of work, and attitude and familiarisation training is an essential requirement. It can be argued that training in any sphere is a matter of applying certain principles and techniques, and whilst this is true, merely 'putting on one day course' on community librarianship for field work staff is not good enough. It should be rather a much more planned approach, identifying specific needs and then using a combination of methods, making use of both internal and external courses and seminars, job training, coaching and counselling and ensuring that staff at all levels are conversant with the necessary skills and knowledge for their new and possibly difficult tasks and duties.

There are some notable examples of training carried out in the field of inner city working and one of the noticeable themes running through this training is the diversity of methods employed. Manchester Cultural Services have in the last few years adopted a system of team librarianship with emphasis on developing the role of the library in the community.

The Manchester area has culturally mixed communities with large Afro-Caribbean and Asian populations in areas of the City. They have appreciated the need for staff to be aware of the pitfalls in serving ethnic minority communities and the City Council has inaugurated a policy of cultural awareness, accompanied by relevant training programmes. Library staff have already attended race awareness courses organised by the Education Department as well as organising their own more professionally based course. This included outside speakers and dealt with areas such as racial bias and the library and racism in books. Following each talk discussion groups examined questions such as 'Do we know how to detect racism in books and other material?' 'Do, we have racist material in our stocks?', 'Should we remove it, or is this censorship?' and Do we need training/ guidelines for future stock selection?' Backing up such courses, professional staff are given different experience of stock selection through regular visits to the appropriate bookshops and suppliers in order to develop their knowledge of such specialisecd material.

Along with other similar library systems Manchester has appreciated the need to ensure that staff at all levels require basic attitude training rather than leaving the whole question of provision to minorities as being the singular responsibility of an ethnic minorities officer, and thereby refusing to acknowledge multi-racial provision as an important area of concern for all members of staff.

Similarly, Derbyshire country Library has accepted the importance of race awareness training, and to this end it has organised courses for both professional staff and assistants, and Tameside Libraries and Arts plans to hold comparable courses, dealing with basic problems such as names, language and communication, and information needs of ethnic minorities.

Birmingham Public Libraries report that there is on-going training in this area, including seminars for both professional staff and assistants on such topics as understanding different cultures and problems associated with communications in ethnic minority work, the latter using the BBC film Cross Talk. They did, some years ago, organise a week's residential course entitled ' Ethnic groups in Birmingham- a background study'. Over thirty members of staff attended from a wide range of departments and levels within the City Library and it was, naturally, a full programme on the study of different ethnic cultures in Birmingham. Speakers were used from outside the library, including representatives from the Community Relations Councils, Community Relations Office, the City Education Department and local groups and associations. Whole sessions were devoted to the various ethnic groups and there were practical exercise as well as films and visits to a mosque, a Sikh temple and a Hindu temple.

Leicestershire Libraries and Information Service, which has a high percentage of ethnic groups, particularly in the City of Leicester, uses both internal and external courses for training its staff in this area. There has been a series of half-day seminars on services to black communities and participation in the Education Department's series, entitled 'Know your neighbour', which comprises visits to various community venues such as temples. The annual intermediate training course for over thirty library assistants also includes work in the ethnic minority communities.

Community information

Another area of service which has developed over the last few years, as mentioned earlier, has been community information. There has been a growing number of nationally and regionally organised courses as well as individual public libraries which have conducted their own internal training. Manchester Cultural Services has arranged seminars for professional staff which stressed the need for co-operation with other related organisations and bodies concerned with disseminating this type of information and speakers included representatives from the Citizens Advice Bureaux, Welfare Rights office and the DHSS.

Birmingham Public Libraries, as with Services to Ethnic Minorities, have arranged a full residential course on community information. Speakers included members of the library staff as well as ones from outside, such as Bradford Libraries, Leeds School of Librarianship, the University of Nottingham, and from specific agencies, groups and bodies within Birmingham (e.g. Citizens Advice Bureaux, the Urban Renewal Department, Voluntary Service Council). It is interesting to note that along with other sessions on this subject there was one on the implication of training in community information. Since this course there has been a City Libraries Management Team Policy Statement on community information which includes notes and overall guidance to staff. An even more useful tool is their community information training package. Packaged training, can form an important adjunct both to job and off-the-job training or even a basis for actually instructing and guiding staff. Birmingham's is an excellent example of packaged training, including functions such as the acquisition and organisation of resources, enquiry work and referral, publicity and promotion of services and a sample training sheet used in the Small Health Library. As is emphasised in the package it is a basis for training, not a substitute for it! There are guides to books and other information which will be of use in enquiry and advice work as well as notes on the use of he index to information and advice service in Birmingham. The sample staff training notes for Small Heath Library are a fairly informal but detailed id to staff who need to know about the basic areas of he community information service. An example is uoted below:

> *3 The card index*
>
> This is housed on the counter by the phone. If we can't answer someone's question immediately this lists other sources of help and information. It also lists all local groups, societies, community centres and associations, residents groups, etc.
>
> If we can't answer someone's question and need to refer them, be as helpful as possible; phone the organisation up and see if they are the right place to send them (people who get shunted form one department to another are likely to give up); perhaps arrange for them to see someone specific so that they have a name to ask for when they get there. If in doubt about where to send someone, phone to Law Centre or Osborne House (under 'Advice Centres' in card index and chock with someone who knows).

Training needs and staff appraisal

In the two chapters so far there has been an emphasise what one could term the 'middle part' of training, or actual execution. Training does not just happen, and that has to be starting and finishing points. Whilst one should never assume that training has been complete it is important that each programme should follow some sort of process. One simple way of examining such a process is through which is known as the Training Cycle.

The assessment or identification of training needs, therefore, must be talked first and foremost, and one should not be lured into the trap of just 'doing some training' on the spur of the moment without first considering who needs training, what it is they need, who will best carry out the instruction and by what methods. There are, of course, organisational as well as individual requirements, for instance the introduction of new routines, procedures or services all have training implications, and it is the job of the library supervisor and training officer to recognise these nee... initially and to consider how they can be fulfilled most effectively. It is all too easy to say that someone will 'pick up the threads as they go along' or 'if they read the Staff Manual it will tell them.' Staff do not respond well to this attitude and in turn this will be reflected in their approach and commitment to their job.

One system which may, if so designed, help in the identification and analysis of needs is that of staff appraisal. This is not particularly widely used in public libraries although there are a few exceptions. Appraisal tends to be regarded with extreme suspicion by staff and trades unions as a means of disciplinary action, either official or unofficial, as well as being a 'big brother' technique of managerial control. The industrial widely, and an important element of this can be to give both supervisor and supervised active encouragement in the planning of training by using appraisal interviews and records to identify needs. It is of course a technique which requires careful handling and needs a great deal of thought and planning as well as commitment and time once the system is operational. It also requires training of all staff concerned; the appraiser and appraisee must ensure unopen and co-operative environment from which both problems and training needs can be identified and handled correctly. Unfortunately this is not easy to achieve.

Some local authorities have adopted appraisal techniques both formal and informal. The Co-ordinating Librarian in Renfrew District Libraries interviews each member of staff once a year to discuss their future needs and requirements. Whiles the system used is not too formal it appears to be a good way of forward planning from which one can extract a great deal of training information. It is also a continuous process, an important point to bear in mind, rather than a stop-part method which will only serve to confuse and dis-illusion staff.

Hampshire Country Library has a staff counselling and career development scheme in operation which takes the form of annual interviews with supervisors. There is an interview summary form completed for each person which is subsequently examined by the Personnel and Training Officer and this provides a good indication of an individual's perception of training needs. One disadvantage reported in this case, however, is the delay in places being obtained on courses run by the central Manpower Service Department when this method of training may have been identified as satisfying a particular need. This can often be a problem in training, particularly when training resources are out of the control of the client department. However, Hampshire at least has made an attempt to get down to analysing needs on a systematic basis, which, unfortunately a great many public library authorities appear not to do.

In a slightly different way Tameside Libraries and Arts participate in an authority-side assessment of needs analysis as part of the annual training plan and budget. Each member of staff receives a Training Needs Assessment form which enables individuals to assist in planning their own training programme. These forms are divided into sections containing further education, in-service/short external courses and practical/other training, When completed, the forms are checked by the appropriate supervisor and ultimately by a senior member of staff. When staff training requirements have been agreed and approved the form is returned to individuals indicating which type of training will be most appropriate.

If completed well, this type of assessment may indicate many areas which will not necessarily be picked up by the usual methods, and could also indicate organisational as well as individual needs. Other public libraries report a much less formal approach to appraisal and identification of needs, preferring to have supervisors identifying those needs on a day-to-day basis. Provided that these supervisors have themselves been instructed and guided, this methods will probably form the bulk of training needs assessment for new library assistants whereby a report is sent by the supervisor to the training officer which assesses their capabilities and identifies weaknesses and further training requirements. Other public libraries have adopted a similar approach for new staff, but in many cases formal training needs assessment appears to stop once he probationary period has been completed.

Overall formal appraisal linked to training does not appear to be a particular or well used technique in public libraries. The examples given above are fairly isolated cases, maybe because of lack of time, but more likely through in built resistance by groups and individuals. However, it might be said in its favour that appraisal need not be ultra-formal, using elaborate systems and complicated forms. Renfrew's system, whilst probably time consuming, will in all probability identify the vast majority of individual's needs over a particular period, in additional to allowing a senior member of staff to have regular chats with staff, thus possibly creating a climate within the system where everyone excepts to be involved in some training on a regular basis.

Coaching and counselling techniques may also be used as a means of identifying gaps in training. These techniques, can assist staff in solving or working through problems by advice rather than taking either a more dictatorial stance on the hand or a 'letting them get on with it' attitude on the other. As mentioned previously, it is a technique being developed by certain public libraries such as Sheffield.

Evaluation

A notoriously difficult area of training is evaluation. It is, to say the least, an inexact science. A great deal of time and effort must be expended in order to ensure that the money and time has been effectively spent. Effectiveness of training can be measured in many ways depending upon the type of instruction used (e.g. course, job-training, programmed learning, etc.) although there appears, even amongst training personnel in public libraries, a natural reluctance to spend a substantial amount of time on it. It is understandable in that many areas of library services are extremely difficult to measures, and staffs' work and training may often be geared to non-measurable standards. For instance, how is one to measure attitude training in a scientific way without spending an inordinate amount of valuable time? It is more likely that certain responses are sought from trainees at the end, or even during, a programme rather than employing a professional firm of training consultants at unacceptable costs! The trainer will hope, in all probability, that the outcome of such training will be a change for the better in attitude as monitored by their supervisor in a working situation.

The popular method of evaluation is the post-course questionnaire, where at least there is an attempt to evaluate the course its (i.e., was it well planned and organised?, were the teaching/learning methods appropriate?, did the course set out to achieve what it purported to achieve?), and with more difficulty, what the trainee learnt and how it may be applied in his/her job in the future. East Sussex Country Council has developed this a little further by a training evaluation and validation questionnaire which is in two parts. Part A, completed before the course by the nominee and supervisor, attempts to determine a little more about the attitude and reasons for attending, including questions such as 'What do you hope to learn from the course?' And 'What difference do you expect their to be in your work performance after the course?'. Part B, Completed by the nominee after the training, requires an immediate evaluation of the course. Trafford Library Service adopted a similar method in their series of supervisory courses using a pre-course questionnaire which attempted to stimulate the trainees' thoughts about the forthcoming training. A fairly full post-course questionnaire, giving plenty of room for comments, and linked to the pre-course questionnaire by using related questions in order to ascertain any change in attitude, was sent one month after the completion of the course. This time lag was carefully predetermined in order that more objective opinions and comments on the training would be forth-coming.

Newcastle City Libraries' assessment of their training programme on the Lending Enquiry Desk was a combination of end of course evaluation seminars and post-course assessment forms. A report on the trainees' comments was complied and sent to their Training Working Group for further consideration.

Another popular methods of evaluation is the post-course report written by the trainee. This is popular not least because it requires little or no thought and effort on the part of the trainer. Whilst it can be useful for stimulating discussion on the contents of the course as an evaluation tool it is of extremely dubious quality, particularly where no guidance has been given to the trainee.

In general there appears to be little activity in evaluation of training by public libraries. It is, as mentioned earlier, a difficult area, often including terminology which is in itself confusing. The Library Association's Guidelines on Training have included Evaluation as one of the sections, written by Alan Gurr, and this, thankfully, is a clear and concise introduction to the subject.

Over the last few years it appears that training in public libraries throughout the country has been patchy. Undoubtedly some library systems do recognise the need to take the matter seriously and have made great strides in the training field. Unfortunately training was a subject much discussed during the 1970s with many courses and meetings organised up and down the country but depressingly at the present time there appear to be other concerns which militate against its development in many systems. However, the Library Association's requirements on licentiateship do seem to have had the necessary impact on training in this particular area and it is hoped that this interest will be maintained and fostered in all levels of staff. As the Working Party on Training indicated, training is not a luxury, but a necessity during good and bad times, whether finance and time are plentiful or scarce.

11

EVALUATING LIBRARY PUBLIC RELATIONS

It is difficult but not impossible. The real problem is that the cost of such measurement may be greater than the cost of the public relations effort itself. To measure the results of a campaign, which attempted to change public attitudes and opinions towards the library service, would require quite sophisticated and expensive research. It would be even more difficult and costly to try and measure the long-term cumulative effects of public relations.

Public relations is an act of faith. One of the functions of PR is to act as an insurance against the future. Thus, a library service wants to keep its public informed, not just for immediate short-term benefits, but also for a future time when it may need their help and support. During my tour of the United States we asked every public relations librarian. 'How do you evaluate your results?' The most common replay to my question can be summed up in the response, 'We hope it does some good'.

Faith and hope, then, play a large part in the PR person's philosophy. There is, however, little room for charity. Library public relations does have to justify itself. Certainly, a library committee, spending rate-payers' money on library publicity and promotion, will want some indication of the possible benefits of PR to the library and the community it serves.

Of course, before any kind of evaluation can be attempted, it is necessary to know what any particular public relations activity was intended to achieve. As we saw from the previous chapter, part of PR planning is to set objectives and targets. No public relations activity should be embarked upon without a clear understanding of what the library hopes to gain from it.

The means by which such objectives might be achieved have been discussed in the earlier part of the book. The precise nature of the 'measure' of their effectiveness will obviously vary with the kind of activity undertaken. In the following paragraphs some possible methods of evaluation are discussed. Some of these have been used by American library organisations and others have been tried by commercial public relations concerns on both sides of the Atlantic. In my view, none of the methods described is rigorous enough to give anything more than a general indication of the success or failure of any particular public relations activity.

Such a lack of precision is not just a problem in library public relations but in public relations in general. As two leading PR consultants write: 'The public relations profession is striving for practical, universally applicable methods of evaluation, but it must be freely admitted that for the time being the practitioner and the management area obliged to put their faith in personal observation and empirical evidence of the many public relations programs which have been followed by good results.'

A number of American libraries have used various forms of media exposure analysis to measure the success of failure of their press and broadcasting relations. Press cuttings are one yardstick by which a librarian can evaluate his or her public relations activities. If press releases consistently fail to be published, it may be that there is something wrong with the nature of the release or that they are being sent to inappropriate newspapers and magazines.

A very simple measure is simply to count the single-column centimeters of coverage received by the library in the press. Though this will tell you little more than that the library received so many centimeters of coverage, such an analysis can usefully be taken further by examining the type of publication in which the library service does, or does not, obtain coverage.

When evaluating radio and television coverage, some libraries in the United States keep a detailed record of all those stations that carry library material, noting the amount of air time devoted to the library service. The report of the one library's Public Relations Department contains an itemised listing of radio and television announcements'. Another library gathers information from local radio and television stations on their usage of library publicity material.

Records can also be kept of the number of people who attend a library promotional event, such as the showing of a library film, though there is some evidence to suggest that the people who attend such events tend already to be well informed about the service or topic being promoted. In general, it is very important to remember that media exposure analysis only shows the extent to which a public relations item has been used by the media. The fact that a library's message has been disseminated does not by any means guarantee that it has any effect.

The success or otherwise of a public relations activity does not just depend on the campaign itself, but also on the audience for it. Even when a library has been successful in 'reaching' the public with a message, people still have to interpret that message for themselves. Individual psychological, sociological, and geographical factors will cause some people to discount, distrust, or simply ignore the message. An individual's selective exposure mechanisms can determine just what information he or she pays attention to, It is not unknown for people to avoid actively some forms of information (if you are a smoker how do you react to anti-smoking campaigns?), while others may be simply apathetic. A number of public information campaigns designed to promote some most worthy causes have floundered because of such audience factors.

Surveys

In exceptional cases, a library service may wish to commission a survey of clients' attitudes before and after a campaign or promotion. Opinion research, is however, likely to be expensive but it is a false economy to attempt to do such work 'on the cheap'. The result obtained from a badly designed questionnaire or poor interviewing are likely to be worse than useless in that they may well be misleading. Personal feedback from clients, councillors, and community leaders may provide information which may be more useful in assessing the library's public standing.

The increase in the use of a library's services following a publicity campaign may be a measure of the effect of a campaign, but not necessarily so. It will require quite sophisticated research techniques to isolate the effects of a campaign from all the other internal and external factors that may, or may not, have led to an increase in the use of service. When attempting to measure the effects of public relations, one must beware of confusing correlation with causation.

With some public relations activities it is possible to encourage audience response directly. For example, a coupon can be include with a publication inviting readers to mail a comment or request to the library. New York Public Library has used this technique to measure the effectiveness of its direct mail publications. This particular method can lead to very biased responses and results need to be interpreted with great caution. Similar techniques can be used to measure the method is to include a write-in competition as part ot the show.

Fund-raiding campaigns may be more directly evaluated by reference to the size of the dollar contributions, though, no doubt, an individual or group donation may also depend on external economic factors.

Research

Research is needed at both the micro and the macro level. There is a need to answer operational questions about such things as the successes or otherwise of a library exhibit, or the extent of press coverage, but also we need to study public attitudes to libraries and to examine the nature of the criticism of library services. We have no way of really knowing if criticisms of library services. We have no way of really knowing if criticisms of library services derive from the services themselves, populist views about public expenditure, or simply- or rather complicatedly-lack of knowledge. It may be that attitudes to a service change with time. Trend studies of attitudes to libraries might help us find out.

Research in this area is not going to provide quick or easy answers but that should not prevent its being carried out. Most of the research that has been done on the effectiveness of library public relations activities has been at the micro. Rather than the macro level.

The British Library Research and Development Department has funded some studies of PR techniques. One based in Newcastle attempted to evaluate the effects of promotional techniques on library use, in particular that is small service points. Investigated direct mail advertising as a method of 'selling' the library. Although both were interesting and well-documented experiments, their results were somewhat inconclusive.

In Sweden, as Greta Renborg has reported, a few attempts have been made to evaluate public relations activities, particularly those aimed at the non-user. In the United States, Sue Fontaine's study was intended 'to examine the state of the art of public relations in selected 'to examine the state of the art of public relations in selected public libraries. "He report does look at evaluation but reflects the lack of rigorous measurement techniques that we have noted elsewhere. The commentary to the tape-slide presentation developed from the study states: 'How do you measure public relations successes or failures? ... It's public opinion that counts. Increased use of the library... and increased support in terms of dollars tell how well we are doing our job.

Also from the United States comes a report of a pilot project to 'illustrate the effectiveness of a tailor-made public relations campaign'. This was centered on Adel Public Library, serving a population of 2.500, and was primary concerned with the effectiveness of library community relations. The public relations officer for the State Library Commission of lows has no doubts about the success of Adel's community relations programme. She reports: 'Hundreds of new users... circulation has increased dramatically.... more funding from he city... organisations are contributing money for a new film projector and screen.. a slide projector has been donated... volunteers renovated the basement.... and a Friends group has been formally organised'. These are very positive results and it is to be hoped that the effect of the campaign is continuing and that such good results can be duplicated elsewhere.

Few librarians have felt able to be so sure about the effects of their public relations efforts because, as we have noted elsewhere, the evaluation of PR is a difficult and expensive task. However, it is also a necessary one. It is essential to evaluate library public relations in order to establish just how far a library such evaluation should be an integral part of the planning processes for future public relations activities.

The evaluation of library services has long been a concern of the Public Libraries Research Group. As part of its current work on public library performance measures, the group has produced a statement on library public relations. This statement, which is reproduced below, is based on an outline submitted to the group by the author.

12

Library Planning, Resources and Staff Training

During a discussion on preparing a staff training session for our Integrated Library System (ILS), a colleague remarked that the Chinese curse "May you live in exciting times," seemed most appropriate. Certainly, implementing an ILS is exciting. With it, however, comes the curse of applying this new, expensive system in a manner that maximises its potential benefits. Indeed, the obligation to meet successfully the short-term and long-term objectives of an ILS are great. Implementation touches the work of nearly all library employees and, like other programs, require library administrators to detail a clearly defined plan. Central to this implementation plan is staff training program that takes into account the considerable human and material resources required.

Background

Recent data from William Saffady and Richard Boss show that there is a substantial market for integrated multi-function library systems. Saffady tallied an estimated 995 integrated systems either installed of contracted for in North American libraries through June 1987 while Boss's statistics for operational systems throughout the world at the end of 1987 reached approximately 2,000 sites. Boss also provides some illuminating numbers showing the volume of turkey sales since the mid-1980's. Saffady points out that over 34% of currently operating systems were installed more than 5 years ago and are consequently, candidates for replacement and that by 1990, over 54% of currently installed systems will be more than 5 years old. The tend is clearly that automated systems are a continuing fact of library administration.

Surely such a level of activity should result in a substantial number of reports on systematic implementation plan in the professional literature. Surprisingly, this is not the case. One may speculate that there are primarily 2 explanations. First, the procurement phase for an ILS is an extraordinary effort marked by uncertainty and linked to funding, local computing support, consortium politics and the sometimes precarious state of the marketplace. So much energy is expended acquiring a system that developing an action plan for implementation lags. Secondly, there is the role played by consultants and vendors. Consultants work with libraries during the procurement phase and their participation usually culminates in negotiating a contract. Advice on implementation may identify concerns such as site preparation, database conversion, training technical staff, system acceptance and library staff training but does not approach the level involvement of the procurement phase. Vendors, on the other hand, are adept at providing technical specifications to install the system but tend to provide painfully little realistic information on the local resources needed to train staff and document and system. Saffady found in his survey that few libraries found the vendor provided training beneficial. In fact, "most considered it marginally acceptable, and some indicated that after the initial session, they, did not bother to schedule their remaining training days". Vendor training was typically supplemented by workshops conducted by library staff members and, overall, that staff training tended to be self-perpetuating, with some sites providing occasional workshops in to meet staff needs. In addition, Saffady relayed the comments from many sites to plan to condense and rewrite the vendor's user manuals which were labeled as "poorly written, contained incomplete and confusing discussions of most system capabilities and omitted many topics."

On the attention given to ILS implementation in the professional literature or in presentation at conferences, most tends to be couched amid caveats or present a farraginous approach. These themes seem to be: beware that changes in internal operations can force organisational changes; beware that automation can impose a powerful psychological presence upon staff; here is what happened to our cataloging/acquisitions/serials/circulation department once automation was introduced.

The number of libraries acquiring an ILS over the part 5 years is a testimony to its value: improved use of the facility; increased operational effectiveness of staff; and better service to constituency groups. Nevertheless, a question remains regarding whether these libraries are receiving the best possible return on the time, staff, and funds invested in their ILS. In an earlier article, the authors presented the theoretical concepts behind the need to develop a systematic staff training program that applies management concepts to the library's overall strategic plan, a vision of how to create and administer implementation of an ILS and how to maintain it within a continuing organisational schemes becomes clear.

Front-end analysis (FEA)

Traditionally, administrators have asked certain questions when implementing an automated system module. Some questions might be: what is the cost? what is the time commitment required of staff to learn the new system? What is the staff's attitude now? What should their attitude be? What specific skills will be needed? What changes will there be in policy and personnel? Problematic with this approach is that it may encourage an administrator's "jumping" to a solution rather than applying a rational model which accurately defines the problem and confirm that it can be addressed through training.

From the authors' experience, a more rational problem solving/training model was defined by Joseph Harless over 20 years ago. He proposed a "Front-end Analysis" (FEA) method that forced the user to think through the underlying conditions or terms creating the "problem" environment and then link solutions to a training model. Harless argued that people perform job tasks incorrectly for one of three reasons: they do not know how to do them; they are prevented from doing them correctly; or that lack the incentive to do them. These concerns must be acknowledged and compared against the overall management plan in order to achieve appropriate results. The authors have adopted a modified form of Harless' FEA problem solving model.

This problem solving model does not preclude using any of the standard "tools" (such as needs assessment instruments, direct observation, client feedback, or actual program monitoring) which library administrators may have found helpful. Focus groups can also be utilised to take advantage of the employee's expertise rather than repressing it. Recent literature such as In Search of Excellence stress the great creative power which can be unleashed when managers and their staffs are able to address problems directly-particularly when there is clear indication that their suggestions will be implemented.

Many library administrators view golf as a healthy and relaxing activity. They fantasise about the joy of walking the links with friends while executing long drives, graceful iron shots, and perfectly placed putts. For all their good feelings about the fame, some library administrators are reluctant to play as frequently and they would like because of real or perceived performance deficiencies. Their game would be more beneficial if their performance level could improve. To improve their game through, our library linksters must first identify specific deficiencies.

How can this be done? One method is to consult outside sources: fellow players, the club pro, or any of the numerous pamphlets, videotapes, or books on the subject. Each of these resources offers a particular perspective on "effective" golf. Another method might be to videotape their drives, chip shots and putting styles. Viewing the tapes in the privacy of their homes, they can compare their actual performance on the golf course with the instructions garnered from the above resources.

These comparisons between desired performance (club pro, in structural materials) and actual performance (friends' observators, videotapes), form the basis of understanding the deficiencies being faced. Perhaps several elements contribute to their problems: poor foot stance, jerking the head, bad grip, and underweight clubs. For each of these contributing factors, our library administrators must determine why that factor is problematic and how to resolve it. For example, poor foot stance may explain why drives are hooking of slicing; jerking the head could be the cause of topping the ball on iron shots; not getting sufficient distance on shorts might be attributable to underweight clubs; and a bad grip could explain why putts are consistently right of the cup. To resolve the undesirable situation those causes must be exposed and addressed.

When our library administrators have completed the first phase of golfing FEA, they will have:

1. Defined the difference between the current situation and the desired state;
2. Identified several major factors contributing to their problems; and
3. Analysed why each factor is significant and determine how to correct it by performance improvement.

The next phase of the FEA involves an Action Plan to reduce/eliminate the contributing factors noted in point 2 above and move toward a solution. An Action plan must be assembled in such a manner that successful implementation of any changes includes reorganisation of resource limitations such as practice time, physical stamina, money, or facilities. It is essential, however, that prior to beginning the action planning mode, a reasonable assessment of resource availability successfully be undertaken. In the authors' view, many well-intentioned training (performance improvement) effects prove fruitless because a realistic assessment has not taken place. When the resource assessment activity has been concluded, the Action Plan can begin by developing specific tactics to address each of the contributing elements identified earlier.

Applying this to our golfing librarian example, our subject may conclude that foot placement is corrected by pointing the tip of the left shoe toward a spot on the back of the club. A bad grip may be corrected by aligning the fingers according to the Palmer Methods before putting. Further, putting may be improved by spending 15 minutes on the putting green before each round. The matter of underweight clubs is obviously not a performance problem and can be corrected by matching the weight of the clubs to problem and can be and weight. From the prior assessment, our subject knows the performance value of a suitable set of clubs and the cost for acquiring them. Another major element of FEA is Harless' strong contention that the value the performance improvement must exceed the costs associated with achieving it. If not, he argues, don't brother to influence the behavior.

With the tactics defined and the resources for needed improvement allocated, the Action plan implementation phase can begin. At this point, adequate preparation needs to be made to assure that reasonable performance reviews are conducted and opportunities to improve/revise training strategies are included in the overall plan. Having exposed a basic FEA through a not-too-serious example, we will now more to a discussion of applying FEA in a more "real-life" setting.

Prior to making any decisions to develop a staff training program at the authors' institution, it was recognised that the best method to assess staff strengths and deficiencies would be by distributing a needs assessment to all staff. A short cover acknowledged the valuable automated system experience that many staff members already possessed. This experience the memo stressed, offered a tremendous resource for developing an effective training program to support implementation. The needs assessment asked staff to help by identifying training techniques that worked for them. This approach gave staff the opportunity to exercise positive control in their new automated environment and potentially lessened possible resistance to the introduction of the new system. By recognising the human resource factors, grassroots support was invited and secured This was proven through the active participation during the training cycle.

For the needs assessment instrument a general section solicited the degree of interest for workshops on such topics as: library automation terminology, computing terminology, various campus computing services, and other topics that staff suggested. Widespread interest in attending a serious of such workshops was expressed. The primary section addresses training and sought to identify how staff had been trained on automated systems in the past. Questions were worded to encourage participation. For example, staff were asked what in their previous training experience did they consider "the single best training techniques and would recommend be used' in our local program. Similarly, they were asked "what would you urge be avoided? ' The responses to the needs assessment were reported in the library's in-house newsletter. The needs assessment revealed that staff overwhelmingly preferred small group training much hands-on experienced. In addition, it was revealed that nearly all had been trained by a supervisor, co-worker, or gained skills osmotically while on-the-job. This lead to the conclusion that good and bad techniques may be practiced and reinforced with each generation of employee. Appropriately, the needs assessment had identified strengths and deficiencies. It was understood that a small group of trainers would be selected from among staff in all departments to develop an in-house training program for the online catalog and cataloging. A plan of action to realise this raised several questions. How can these persons best be prepared for the task? What library resources will be required. Are there external resources available to support the project? what is the proposed timetable?

The first step taken to organise the trainers into a "focus group" and enlist the aid of a training specialist from the University's personnel office. The training specialist lead the focus groups through a series of workshops exploring adult learning theory, competency measurement, listening and questing skills, developing training objectives and program design. Through the focus group approach, the trainers framed their past learning experiences on automated systems around sound staff training techniques. A basic level of knowledge was acquired in a positive environment while promoting enthusiasm for the project.

As the focus groups met to hone their training skills and develop a staff training program, administrative support was garnered by drafting a training statement that enlisted the support of administrative staff from department heads (middle managers) up to the director. This statement centralised administrative control for staff training on the new system and established the successful execution of the training program as a library goal. It eliminated potential roadblocks by having each department head agree to support the time trainers were required to spend in the focus groups and to commit additional staff time for training and individual practice. The training statement was an important step to ensure that library staff would not find themselves in the confusing position of serving two masters.

Front-End analysis keeps the training officer over mindful that the in -house staff training program must be flexible and offer numerous approaches to correct observed or possible performance deficiencies. When one approach does not work as well as expected, an alternative is identified. For example, introductory training for staff on the system's technical service module was based on the behavior modeling approach advocated by Kay Tylter Abella. This approach recommends giving training step-by-step instructions, demonstrations, discussions on technique, trial exercises, and feedback. Unfortunately, this method proved extremely time consuming and repetitious for the trainers. As an alternative, a self-paced workbook with an online training file was prepared for staff. While one-on one training is still available if requested, the workbook has been an enormous boom to system trainers who can now apply their skills to advanced training for a select group. In addition, a more general approach has been developed to provide staff training or information on a variety of system related to topics. A series of 20-30 minute presentations have been prepared (usually as "brown bag lunches") tc provide general information. Topics include system hardware, software, and telecommunications; the MARC record and its relation to the local system; the local system's architecture and file structure; the workings of specific modules, like circulation and system security. Several of these topics were listed on the original needs assessment and other topics can be developed.

Time analysis

As an example of the commitment a library administrator can expect to make to in-house staff training on a automated system, a time analysis of the authors' initial efforts is outlined. This first program was to train all library staff on the new system's online catalog. With hindsight, some aspects might have been conducted differently. Nevertheless, the organisational structure of this training program has withstood the test of time and three years later serves as the model for subsequent training projects. The steps listed below detail the elements of this initial program and approximate the total number of hours contributed by each participant category. For convenience, the following codes are used: CS = Campus specialist; STO= Systems training officer; L= Librarians; S = Support staff.

1. Pre-planning: system, training officer and campus specialist review responses to the needs assessment and draft a plan of action which includes steps, timetable and resource requirements. CS: 10 hours; STO: 5 hours.

2. System training officer presents training concept to other library administrators by outlining focus group concept, training plan, time commitment, and administrative commitment. STO: 1.5 hours

3. Trainers are appointed and their role is examined to them. A total of 11 staff members, including 4 librarians and 7 senior support staff will work with systems training officer. 4L: 1 hour; 7S: 1.75 hours

4. Systems training officer and campus specialist plan workshop 1 for focus groups, Involves selecting reading material, discussion topics, scheduling, preparing materials for distribution, CS: 10 hours; STO: 5 hours.

5. Workshop 1: A 1.5 hour workshop discusses the difference between teaching and training, training techniques and approaches, and adult learning

theory, CS: 2 hours; STO: 2 hours; 4L: 6 hours; 7S: 10 hours

6. Systems training officer and campus specialist prepare for workshop II; trainers read and prepare to discuss 2 articles. CS: 5 hours; STO: 4 hours; 4L: 8 hours; 7S: 14 hours.

7. Trainers attend vendor training session on online catalog and begin practicing on test database. STO: 10 hours; 4L: 24 hours; 7S: 42 hours.

8. Workshop II: topics include skills acquisition, questioning techniques, answering techniques, one-on-one training and designing training sessions. Focus group break down into smaller groups to develop a syllabus, user aids, exercises, scheduling procedures, and promotional materials. CS: 2 hours; STO: 1.5 hours; 4L: 6 hours; 7S: 10.5 hours

9. Materials from small groups are drafted fro other focus group members to reviews. 4L: 20 hours; 7S: 35 hours

10. Focus group meets to review, revise, and formalise syllabus, user aids and exercises. Training sessions dates are reserved, announced to all staff, and scheduled. STO: 4 hours; 4L: 8 hours; 7S; 25.5 hours

11. Trainers rehearse. 4L: 4 hours; 7S; 7 hours

12. Training begins: 1-2 trainers per session; 8 one hour slots per week over 4 weeks. STO: 4.5 hours; 4L: 15 hours; 7S: 25.5 hours

13. System training officer prepares and distributes evaluation questionnaire which is sent to all library staff. STO: 3 hours

14. Trainers review returned questionnaire and

discuss possible training enhancements based on responses. STO: 1 hour; 4L: 4 hours; 7 S: 7 hours.

15. Workshop III: Focus group reviews overall experience and long them training projects. STO: 1.5; 4L: 6 hours; 7S: 10.5 hours.

13

INFORMATION TECHNOLOGY AND ADMINISTRATION

The relation of government to information technology and civilisation is only a small part of overall government activities. We do not describe here the aspirations of nations or heads of state, not matters of defense, nor even the gamut of social and cultural activities. We shall deal with some of these indirectly, but only as these areas necessarily come to our attention in dealing with matters that involve information technology and civilisation directly.

Whether not market forces are officially recognised, in all nations they have played—and will continue to play—a major role in advancing information technology and in enhancing the quality as well as the quantity of information-oriented products and services. Even in nonsocialist economies, there are areas in which market forces are weak or do not function satisfactorily. Therefore, government can—and should—play a leading role in these areas by providing assistance, removing impediments, and coordinating related activities, always in concert with market forces and always helping, not hindering, so as to maximise the benefits of information technology to society while keeping its negative impacts as low as possible.

The means by which public ends are accomplished differ tremendously among countries. In some countries, Most authority and action stem from central government. In other, many of the most important functions of government are at a state or even a locale. Many public functions are carried out through private organisations and autonomous bodies, as in licensing of artisans and the setting of technological and industrial standards is carried out by private organisations in many countries.

Areas in which government assistance is crucial are basic research in information technology, where the cost and risk are rapidly increasing, and assurance of availability of information resources and information-oriented societal infrastructure, where market forces do not function.

Areas in which the government should remove impediments are the regulation of information services where the convergence of service modes is in progress and the promotion of greater social responsibility for the protection of privacy and the great need for security.

Government should work for closer coordination of basic research in universities, in government institutions, and in industrial laboratories. The competitive and cooperative aspects of information services should be carefully balanced so as to utilise limited resources of money and human energy efficiently. Standardisation by governments or industrial associations should be encouraged in order to ensure the maximum compatibility of equipment consistent with future progress of information technology. Information supplies and vendors should be organised to promote the flow of information while ensuring its integrity. And all of the above activities should be carried out in concert with the rest of the world.

This chapter explores the problems government faces in connection with information technology and describes the role that the authors hope the government will play.

The support of research and development

Governments in many countries support research and development in information technology in various ways. They provide almost all the research funds available to universities and government institutions in these areas. Government also help to support research and development activities in industries through purchases of high-technology products and through research contracts, low-interest loans, and tax incentives, Some government promote collaboration between universities, government laboratories, and private industries by providing financial or other assistance to joint projects.

Research and development in information technology are becoming extremely costly and risky because of the technological alternatives to be explored and because of the increasing complexity and scale of these technologies. Industries with information-oriented products increase expenditures for research and development year after year. Major industries in the world are now spending as much as 5 to 10 percent of their sales for research and development. However, the government expenditure in support of research and development tends to remain unchanged or even to decline because of severe constraints on national budgets. As we see it, the government share of this effort is diminishing.

Nevertheless, there are important areas in which

the government most play a major role. Basic research is one of these areas. Because of increasing cost and risk, industries tend to invest most heavily in applied research and development rather than in basic research, while universities and government institutions continue to suffer from a shortage of financial support. The government should encourage industries by sharing the cost and risk of basic research and should reactivate basic research at universities and government institutions. In particular, due attention should be played to supporting basic research activities in small and medium-sized high-technology firms, from which many useful innovations have come and where the hazards as well as the rewards of risk taking are particularly large.

The government should also promote closer cooperation between universities, government institutions, and industrial laboratories in carrying out basic research in information technology by organising and partly financing joint projects, This helps academia to confront reality and helps industry to draw wisdom from academia. In a few industrialised countries, small-and medium-sized high-technology firms have been in close contact with academia and have thereby contributed significantly. Such association should be introduced and enhanced in many other countries by the removal of organisational and societal constraint where necessary.

There are many areas in which market forces do not necessarily function to promote research and development. Societal infrastructure is one typical area. Information technology will help significantly in strengthening the societal infrastructure. However, this area is not very lucrative for industry, because the beneficiaries generally cannot pay the cost. Government initiative in research and development will be particularly important in these areas, even where commercial ventures may later play an important role. If important areas, such as 'agriculture and mining, lag in productivity, the government should help them by supporting appropriate research. Better information on weather or on geological structures may lead to higher productivity. Research and development for the information of such sectors should be promoted by the government when internal motivation in not strong enough. Considering the fact that information technology is an indispensable tool for extending knowledge and developing and conserving the culture of human beings, the government should also pay more attention to research and development in this area.

On the other hand, the government should be very careful in supporting industries where market forces are strong enough, because such support may hamper free competition in the marketplace and may be wasteful as well.

The organisation of society is based on rules—some agreed upon, others more formal and enforced by governmental action—to protect the society from adverse activities. Codes of ethics, constitutions, and laws have been issued from time to time, an early and fundamental set of laws is the Code of Hammurabi, issued by the great king of Bablonia around 2000 BC. The inscription of this code was found on a block of black diorite in 1901. The Code of Hammurabi is of particular interest because of its relation to technology. Specifically, it includes liability clauses and penalties to regulate house builders. These same regulations might have remained effective throughout the 2000-year span of the Babylonian Empire, since in ancient times, technological innovation was not as rapid as it is today.

In the present world, technological change is often so fast that policy makers cannot understand its implications and adaptively change their regulatory measures. In the area of information technology in particular, where the pace of technological innovation is accelerating and where the convergence of service modes is in rapid progress, policy makers have difficulties in modifying their regulatory policies.

One of the fundamental problems in regulatory policy making in a rapidly changing technological and societal environment is how to product the interest of the public while attaining the maximum possible freedom for private citisens, corporations, and other entities.

Telecommunications and the use of radio waves have been regulated to effectively utilise limited resources for the benefit of all citizens equally and without discrimination. Postal service and telecommunication are also regulated for the protection of privacy, whereas newspapers, journals, books, motion pictures, and radio and television programmes are under far less regulation in most of the democratic countries, in order to encourage a free flow of information and to ensure freedom of expression and the right to know.

The Principle may be basically correct. The problem is that when the convergence of service modes is rapidly dismantling barriers between traditionally regulated and unregulated services, it is increasingly difficult to observe this principle. Specifically, the convergence of modes leads to the need to reorganise regulations. Without such reorganisation, the benefit which information technology is bringing cannot fulfill the diversifying needs of our society; it becomes impossible to decide who can provide which service under what regulation.

Telecommunication service has been provided in almost all countries under national or regional monopoly and under tariff control by the government. The reason is that if telecommunication service is left entirely in the hands of market forces, service in pursuit of profit tends to concentrate in large cities and heavily populated districts rather than in remote, rural villages and sparsely populated districts, Lower rates and better service will be available in the former whereas the latter will suffer higher rates and less service and, ultimately, no service at all. To avoid this, unified tariffs must be set so that each citizen, regardless of where he or she lives in a country, can receive the same basic level of service under the same rate structure.

To maintain the service, an operating agency has to subsidise its loss in a mote villages populated districts by its profits in large cities and heavily populated districts hence, national or regional monopoly has been granted to the common carrier to prevent competition known as cream skimming. Cream skimming in profitable areas makes it difficult for a common carrier to subsidise its loss in less profitable areas. The case of massage switching. If message switching is considered a part of telecommunication service, information processing firms may be regulated or may possibly be prohibited from providing message switching if, on the other hand, message switching is considered part of information processing service, the common carrier may be permitted to provide information processing service or may be prohibited from doing so in order to avoid competition with information processing firms.

The views of policy makers in the world are now split, reflection the situations in their own countries. In some countries in particular where the common carrier is one of the government sectors or is owned by the government, message switching by information processing firms is prohibited or regulates, while information processing by the common carrier is permitted with certain restrictions. In other countries, where common carriers are privately owned and where antitrust and competition are considered of prime importance, message switching by information processing firms is permitted, while information processing by common carrier is prohibited. While no single solution has been found, it is clear that neither of the above solutions is ultimately satisfactory, because each jeopardises the benefit of convergence of telecommunication and information processing services.

We now arrive at issues of competition. If information processing firms are permitted to provide message switching service and the common carrier is permitted to provide information processing service, can they compete properly and thereby bring better services to the public" Probably not. Because common carriers are huge entities that provide basic telecommunication service under regulated monopoly, they may be able to subsidise their information processing service by the profits they gain through basic tale communication Service. Then how about separating message switching from basic telecommunication service and permitting the information processing firms and the common carriers or their subsidiaries to compete." Some may still argue that competition will be hampered because, to provide value-added services as message switching and related new services are called transmission facilities have to be leased from the common carrier.

Puzzled policy makers may then think that basic telecommunication service should be deregulated so that such service can be provided by others, including information processing firms and their subsidiaries. This brings the dispute back to its very beginning. Can we leave all telecommunication service solely in the hands of market forces and yet ensure that basic telecommunication service will be provided equally everywhere in a country? and what service is basic-that which our parents had, that which is common now, or that which out sons and daughters will demand? Policy makers are facing an enormous Gordian Knot that even an Alexander the Great might find difficult to cut in twine.

This is only one of the many problems that policy makers are facing. Another is the use of an additional channel piggy-backed on a television channel. There is no serious problem if the additional channel is used to supplement the main television programme by making if stereophonic or bilingual or by superimposing characters relative to the main programme, perhaps for use by the deaf. If, however, the additional channel is used independently of the main, television programme is violated by an additional programmes that may express different views. If a newspaper company is permitted to use the additional channel for facsimile delivery, will this be considered control of multiple media? Under what condition can the user of the additional channel be licensed?

Broadcasting satellites present still another set of problems. Traditionally, the reallying of television programmes from a key station to local distribution stations is regulated as a part of telecommunication service. Now, a broadcasting satellite programmes to be received directly by television viewers by means of rooftop antennas. If a local broadcasting station received the programmes from the satellite by means of a large antenna (which ensured better quality) and distributed them, would this violate the traditional regulation? In a country where telecommunications, radio wave broadcasting, and cable broadcasting are under separate regulation, how can policy makers regulation, how can policy makers regulate a television network that consists of a key station that transmits a variety of programmes over a broadcasting satellite and a number of local stations that selectively receive these programmes and distribute them over cables? How about as new information vendor that provides a variety of audio, data, and video information by way of a satellite for direction reception and local distribution?

The answers to most of these questions remain to be worked out. What is clear now is that the present regulatory framework is far less than adequate to keep up with the increasing pace of innovation in information technology and the diversifying needs of our society, and that a through understanding of technological and societal implications is urgently needed so that policy makers can update the regulatory framework effectively.

Basically, competition in the marketplace brings benefits to society. In fact, since the regulation on the connection of user owned terminals to the telecommunication network was removed or alleviated, a great variety of terminals with higher performance and lower cost have appeared on the market. Although this is one in part to the emergence of micro-processors, it should be acknowledge that the deregulation of so-called foreign attachments stimulated competition in the marketplace and there by brought into use private automatic board exchanges with new business features, wood processors with text-transmission capability, facsimile terminals of various speeds and time-sharing system (TSS) terminals for switched connection over telephone and data networks.

Competition is good when the competing parties have sufficient resources of money and manpower. Competition, however, leads to a poorer result if the resources available to the competitors are limited or scarce. Telecommunication service, which requires enormous resources for research, development, implementation, and operation, may be one of the examples of the latter category. If a number of firms freely compete in basic telecommunication service in one country, resources available in that country may be divided up, and as a result, the firm that provides the cheapest and worst service, only to show that Gresham's law is still valid. The resources available differ from country to country. Some policy makers may think that their countries can afford such competition and avoid catastrophe. Others may be no single solution to this problem.

Competition also presents problems for broadcasting services. In countries where public broadcasting coexists with commercial broadcasting it has become increasingly difficult to keep public broadcasting competitive. This is particularly true for a public broadcasting agency that supports itself solely by subscription fees because it wants to avoid government intervention in programming. The fact is that the subscription fees of a public broadcasting agency cannot keep up with inflation, while the income of commercial broadcasting companies surpasses inflation because of the shift of advertising from nonelectronic to electronic media. It seems clear that an unsubsidised public broadcasting agency can no longer compete effectively with commercial broadcasting companies. Should nongovernmental public broadcasting be left to fade away? Probably not.

Some policy makers may then think that the government should collect charges from commercial broadcasting companies for the use of radio waves (as it traditionally does in cases of private use of public properties) and use the money to subsidise public broadcasting. Commercial broadcasting companies may naturally object to this as an abuse of power, and the public broadcasting agency may also be reluctant to receive such support because of fear of possible government intervention in its programming.

What is clear at this point is that although completion is a very powerful driving force, it is not the only tool for the betterment of our society. Another tool to which we must pay more attention is cooperation. Cooperation may play a more important role than competition where resources are severely contained. Instead of dividing up limited resources, competing parties may be able to share the resources through appropriate cooperation in accordance with their objectives, functions, and localities. Cooperation between common carries and information processing firms in setting up joint ventures may better promote value-added telecommunication service in its research, development, implementation, and operation. Commercial broadcasting companies may contribute funds, in accordance with their own will, in setting up a nongovernment foundation to support a public broadcasting agency without any strings attached.

However, cooperation is very difficult to accomplish because of the conflict of interest between participating public agencies, private companies, and government sectors. Antitrust laws, which have a dominant power in most of the industrialised countries often work to against cooperation. Powerful insight, motivation, and enthusiasm on the part of government as well as among participating parties are necessary to bring an converging information services.

When human beings began to trade goods, they realised that "Measuring others' corn by their own bushels" dot not work. Measurement is one of the earliest examples of standardisation in human society. In the past, a number of standards have been established for a great, variety of items and procedures, ranging from utensils in a farmer's kitchen to protocols at a royal court. Such standards permit social activities to be carried out smoothly.

Standardisation has proved to be a very difficult task, attempts at standardisation field because of their impracticality. Some standards were found useful, and some of them still survive. The metric system is one example, despite the fact that its basic unit of length has been found to differ from the one forty-millionth of the circumference of the globe it was originally intended to represent.

As modern technology has been rapidly introduced into society, and as societal activities in the world have been more closely knit, a number of international standards have been established. In the area of information technology, the IEC (International Electrotechnical Commission), which recommends standards for electrical equipment and components, was founded in 1906 by Lord Kelvin and others. The ITU (International Telecommunication Union), which recommends standards for telegraph, telephone, data, and radio wave communication was founded in 1865 as the International Telegraph Union. The ISO (International Standards Organisation), which recommends standards for everything else, including computers, was founded in 1946.

By virtue of the efforts of these international

organisations, all telephones in the world can be connected to each other and television programmes can be exchanged by broadcasters throughout the world. However, this does not mean that there is only one standard for telephone systems or for television systems. Rather, the world now has a few different standards for these systems that reflect locality and evolutionary process. These standards are made compatible in order to make interconnection possible. Compatibility is achieved by an interface that convert from one standard to another. Interface units can be very simple or very complex, depending on the difference of standards. If we have n standards to be made compatible, we generally need n(n-1)/2 interfacing units of different types. Having one standard is clearly the best: a few may be tolerable if compatibility can be attained easily, but having many leads to disaster.

Standardisation of the hardware and software of information technology is extremely important because telephone sets, terminals, transmission lines, and switching centers are always connected in networks, and, increasingly, computers and data base are connected to such networks. To permit information to be transmitted and received between these network components, interfaces should be agreed upon, clearly defined, and as possible.

Standardisation is very difficult for a number of reasons. First the pace of innovation in information technology is very fast. A standard set too early may jeopardise future innovation: set too late, it never becomes operational. Second, standardisation is required to cover not only hardware but also software. That is, computer programmes and the like. A very large amount of software at each switching center has to be standardised in order to attain economy of scale and ease of maintenance. To permit communication between terminals and computers. Software standard known as a communication protocol has to be implemented. Generally, to operate and to interconnect equipment that has higher intelligence. More software has to be standardised.

Third, new products tend to have diversified specifications, since they are designed by competing private industries. This makes it particularly difficult to establish a single standard in such areas as computers, terminals, and video packages, where market forces are powerful and new technologies are continually emerging.

Fourth, conflicts of interest may occur between countries or groups of countries in trying to establish a single standard. For instance, three standards-namely, NTSC, PAL, and SECAM-exist for colour television broadcasting. This results in the use of Complicated interfaces for format conversion when an exchange of programmes is required. For the digital hierarchy for multiplexing digital signals, three standards exist, which may require costly interfaces for future interconnection. But settling on a single standard would benefit some more than others, so there are problems of fairness and politics in addition to the technical side of these issues.

Standardisation in information technology requires a great deal of collaboration and compromise between governments, common carries, and industries in the world. It also requires a through understanding of the state of the art as well as a far reaching insight into the future by the all the participants, not only those from academia and those who represent users. Governments should assist and encourage, not hamper, co-operative activities to bring better standards to the world. What in encouraging is that despite two world wars and other international conflicts in the past, the standardisation activities of the world have continued and are even accelerating in recent years. Standardisation is perhaps one of very few areas of international activity in which countries, industries, and individuals of diversified backgrounds and interests can think and act constructively and co-operatively for the good of humanity.

Information supply and distribution

The repertoire of information services has been extended from the transmission and switching of information to the processing of information and, then, to the providing of information. In other words, new information services have much affinity with broadcast service, in which the quality and quantity of the information to be provided is the most crucial factor for success or failure. Information collection, processing, and formation, however, require a great deal of effort.

For instance, a data base for bibliographic information retrieval requires that many scientific papers be collected from many professional journals over many years, abstracted and indexed, entered through a keyboard into a computer store in machine-readable form, retrieved upon request, and updated in accordance with new issues, corrections, and other changes. Very few professional institutions can afford to do this by themselves, especially when the information has little commercial value. Therefore, building such data bases requires government assistance, at least until the data base becomes commercially valuable.

Various sectors of the government collect enormous amounts of data for their administrative use. These data are invaluable as industrial, agricultural, economic, and social indicators for business people, economists, sociologists, and many others. In some countries, where a freedom of information law has been enacted, the government data have been made available to the public to the extent that no infringement on privacy and national security occurs. This not only promotes economic and societal progress in broader terms but also encourages information services to use government data by sorting, merging, collating, and processing to fit their customer's needs. In other counters, however, the governments seldom provide the data they own to the public, so that information services suffer a serious lack of materials. Considering the fact that economic and societal activities are increasingly information oriented, governments should be urged to provide their data to the public as much as possible in order to promote economic and societal progress and to help information services sustain their businesses. Considering the importance of the integrity of date, governments should also agree to validate their data as accurately as possible and to make quotations as detailed as possible. For the same reason, information services are required to be very careful in processing data so as not to provide biased or erroneous data to the public.

Information is an invisible commodity. Lake visible commodities, it requires an appropriate distribution mechanism in order to reach end users. The government, therefore, should assist information vendors in developing their distribution channels through computer networks, videotex, teletext, and means. Those who provide information should permit information vendors to have access to their information resources without hindrance. Government assistance seems desirable and necessary for the dissemination of scientific and technological information. Which has little immediate commercial value but is of decisive importance in extending knowledge.

The government should also provide assistance for the formation of information resources for education and improved welfare. For instance, computer, -aided. Instrumation (CAI) systems require that highly sophisticated teaching programmes be produced by close collaboration between experienced educators and talented software produces. Therefore, the government should assist and encourage highly experienced educators to become familiar with computer usage and thereby better co-operator with software producers.

Information resources, especially information in machine-readable form, are unevenly distributed on earth. As a result, many countries suffer from a significant imbalance in information flow, with larger inflow smaller outflow. The government of such countries many think that the flow should be brought into balance by restricting inflow through a custom duty or other berries. This, however, is not the right solution, because such action makes such countries even more information poor. Rather, the government should exert more effort to build up its own information resources so as to increase the information flow out of the country.

Information flow into a country may bed disturbed if that country has no privacy-protection law, because countries supplying information may feel that the privacy of their people may be infringed in that country. The government of such a country is therefore urged to enact a protection-of privacy law (or laws for different areas of application) together with a freedom-of information law, in concert with other countries, so as not to obstruct information flow, which is vital for the progress of mankind. It may be worth noting that the Organisation for Economic Cooperation and Development (OECD) and the Council of Europe have agreed on guidelines on the protection of privacy for the framing of national polices and legislation in harmonised way.

Information technology is a powerful tool for enhancing societal infrastructure, revitalising traditional industrial sectors, extending knowledge, and enriching. Human culture. However, private sectors are generally incapable of paying the cost for the implementation and operation of such information-oriented systems. Beneficiaries of societal infrastructure generally take the benefits for granted and are reluctant to bear the cost -or are incapable of doing so.

Thus the government should provide financial support for information-oriented societal infracture, not only for its development, but also for its operation. The government should be aware of regional differences in the need for such infrastructure, and should distribute systems properly. The government should also encourage local communities and professionals to participate actively in implementing and operating the societal infrastructure so as to service the community better.

The government system itself is a most important societal infrastructure. Tremendous amounts of statistics that have been collected independently in many government sectors often overlap and are sometimes found to be inconsistent or misinterpreted. A very large number of documents produced for administrative purpose are validated, circulated, and filed inefficiently and inconsistently. Administrative information tends circulate through the government system with much delay, and delay hampers decision making. The government should make full use of information technology to make its own system more comprehensive, more efficient, and less costly.

The success of the information-oriented infrastructure depends on the existence of a powerful telecommunication network that can provide telephone service and data, services nationwide and also in remote rural areas. Government can therefore foster the expansion and evolution of the telecommunication network.

The government should also assist traditional industrial sectors in improving productivity and working conditions by use of information technology. The need for assistance seems greatest in such industrial sectors as agriculture, in which market forces are an inadequate stimulus of innovation and upon which the basic needs of human survival are so dependent. For many other industrial sectors, where automation by means of industrial robots and process-control computers is displacing skilled workers and where needs for software are rapidly increasing, the government should provide assistance for continuing education and retraining to provide a smooth shift of the displaced work force to information-oriented jobs.

In view of the fact that number of qualified scientists and engineers is quite limited and that the knowledge gained in the past is quickly becoming obsolete' because of the rapid progress of information technology, it is particularly important to have a comprehensive system for continuing education so that scientists and engineers can keep up with their arts over a lifetime. However, continuing education has been provided mainly be large industries. Small industries-and large industries that are in financial difficulty -cannot afford to support continuing education. The government should therefore encourage universities and other educational institutions to provide continuing-education programmes on the campus or on industries premises by providing financial and other assistance.

Last, but not least, the government should increase its financial support to the use of information technology to extend and preserve our scientific and cultural heritage. Research activities in astronomy, geophysics, oceanography, biology, and all areas of the natural sciences should be encouraged by adequate financing and by establishment of information-oriented research facilities. Research institutions and museums for archaeology, anthropology, and the arts should be armed with information technology so as to better understand and preserve invaluable cultural gifts from our ancestors. Artists should be encouraged to use information technology in their work. Researchers in natural sciences, social sciences, and humanities should be provided with ample information resources through sustained government support in building and updating data bases for a great variety of disciplines.

Societal receptivity

When Prometheus stole fire from heaven and gave it to mankind, Seus sent Pandors to earth with her box of evils. Since then, human beings have used fire in many ways to improve their way of life. However, the evils that escaped from Pandora's box have crept into the human mind and have led to the abuse of that tool, fire, to devastate civilisation. Like fire-and like all other technologies—information technology is a tool. It is a powerful too, the extent to which is used for good or for the bad of humanity is up to human beings themselves.

In the past, possibilities of abusing technology were often overbooked. Technologists tend look for the potential for use rather than abuse, and social scientists and humanists have found difficulties in understanding implications of technology in general. The public has been reluctant to admit that the human mind can be infected by the evils that crept out of pandore's box. Technology assessment was an important step toward clarifying the situation.

Through the joint efforts of technologists and sociologists, technology assessment analyses all the conceivable positive and negative impacts of a technology and provides alternatives to alleviate the negative impacts. Unfortunately, technology assessment does not always provide reasonable alternatives, because the options that alleviate negative impacts of a technology sometimes diminish its positive impacts. Let us take a very simple and years-old technology, a knife, as an example.

A knife has many positive uses, but it also has definite negative potential. When put to evil purpose, a knife may hurt or kill someone. Were the public to feel that the technology of knives was incomplete and unacceptable technological solution might be found? Would it be possible to pick up unusual activity occurring in the mind of a knife owner by using a lie detector, an encephalograph, or some other electronic instrument, and, by using a microprocessor, find evil intent and then electronically lock the owner's knife in its sheath? Enforcement of such a technological option would totally destroy the benefit of a knife by increasing its cost by at least several thousand times. Besides, the invasion of privacy that such a monitoring system might allow would be unacceptable to many people.

Nevertheless, technology assessment is useful in showing the public the positive and negative impacts of a technology together with .its alternatives and also in encouraging people to think sensibly and to make reasonable choices. Through public participation of this sort, people may be provided with the opportunity of understanding a technology and constructing their own ethical standards or means for avoiding it abuse.

It must be admitted, however, that in the past, public participation often ended in rejection of the technology because of lack of understanding on the part of the public of the need for the technology and the necessary for trade-offs in meeting that need. The government should therefore, explain very clearly the societal needs cf technology when inviting the public to participate in assessment.

The government is also requested to take necessary steps in the areas where the negative impacts are apparent. Among other things, government should take necessary measures to protect the privacy of individuals in regard to the automatic processing of personal data. First, the personal data should be scored and used for specific and legitimate purposes, should be checked for accuracy and updated when necessary, and should be preserved in an identifiable from for no longer than the period required for the purpose. Second, personal data revealing racial origin, political or religious background, health, or criminal convictions should not be processed automatically unless an appropriate safeguard is provided by law. Third, appropriate security measures should be taken for the protection of personal data against accidental or unauthorised destruction as well as against unauthorised access, alternation, or dissemination. Fourth, any person should be entitled to know who controls the file in which his or her personal data is stored, to obtain at reasonable intervals and without excessive delay or expense the information stored in the life, and to ask rectification or erasure of such data if these have been processed contrary to the above principles.

Protection of the automatic processing of personal data is just one aspect of a larger issue. Personal data files that are not processed automatically should also be protected in a similar way Protection should also be extended to cover information relating to groups of persons, associations, foundations, private companies, and other entities.

To make such protection effective, the security and reliability of data files and computers should be maintained at the highest level possible. Technologies for enhancing the security and reliability of information systems, have an important role in this respect. At the same time, authorisation of access to data files, alternation of data files, and dissemination of the contents of data files should be placed under strict administrative control. Technological and organisational means will need to be strengthened in view of the fact that "computer crime" is of growing concern. Reliability is a major concern Reliability is a major concern not only for personal data files but also for all of the information systems that are so deeply involved in almost all aspects of societal activities. Any real function or outage of information systems may endanger human life or health, cause serious destruction of industrial plants or the environment, or result in great financial loss. Although the reliability of information systems has already reached an extremely high level, every effort must be expend to enhance reliability even further. At the same time, the government should play a leading role in establishing and enhancing liability coverage and backup safeguards, in concert with the activities in private sectors, because no system can be made absolutely failure-free.

International implications

Clearly, we are living in an age of mutual dependence. The world is so closely knit together that any adverse activity occurring in any part of the world seriously and immediately disturbs the rest of the world. seriously and immediately disturbs the rest of the world. Nevertheless, the countries in the world are different from each other in their cultural, religious, ideological, political, industrial, economic, and other backgrounds. Therefore, governments should pay due attention to the differences in backgrounds when setting up national policies. At the same time, governments should take positive steps towards promoting mutual understanding between countries and cooperatively solving mutual problems.

Information technology presents a number of problems as well as benefits to government in this respect. In the preceding sections, we have observed several instances in which the government is obliged to take into account the international implications of information technology. The government should promote international cooperation in basic research in information technology as well as in research and development for information of societal infrastructures to attain more efficient use of monetary and human resources in the world. However, the government should be very careful in supporting a particular industrial sector where market forces are powerful, because this may disturb free competition in the world market.

When a government restructures its regulatory policy, it should consider compatibility with the regulatory policies of other government so as not to disturb the international flow of information. The government should encourage cooperation of information services not only within its country but also in the international scene, especially in the use of domestic and regional satellites. When assisting standardisation activities, the government should encourage all the participating parties to settle, if possible, on a common standard, and it should urge its public and private sectors to conform with the standard so as not to hamper the international flow of goods and services.

When assisting the formation of data bases and information-distribution mechanisms within its country, the government should cooperate with other government to increase and balance the transborder information flow. The government should enact freedom-of information laws and protection-of-privacy laws in conformity with those of other governments so as to increase international information flow while protection the privacy of the people in the world. The government should provide technology and experience to other governments for promoting scientific knowledge and preserving cultural heritages.

The Prime mover for the progress of the world is fair competition and thoughtful cooperation among countries. Information technology provides unprecedented means of mutual understanding and thereby promotes cooperation among world communities. In the present world of mutual dependence, governments should thoroughly understand the implications of information technology and fully utilise its benefits for the betterment of world society.

INDEX